Why Pool Hustlers Win!!

Learn to Beat the Sharks

Allan P. Sand,
PBIA Certified Instructor

ISBN 978-1-62505-217-9

Print 6x9

ISBN 978-1-62505-531-6

eBook format

Published by Billiard Gods Productions.

Santa Clara, CA 95051

U.S.A.

For the latest information about books and videos, go to:
http://www.billiardgods.com

Acknowledgements

I want to thank my parents, Edmund and Bernadette Sand, who encouraged my interesting in the sport of billiards.

Table of Contents

WELCOME 1
    How Sharking Works.. 2
    Life Examples of Sharking 3
MAJOR SHARKS 4
    Accusations.. 4
    Alzheimer's 6
    Back & Forth 8
    Bad Shot Commentary 10
    Bellyacher.. 12
    Bigmouth.. 14
    Boring 16
    Cell Phone 18
    Clothes & Accessories 20
    Compliments.. 22
    Consoling.. 24
    Cripple Yourself 26
    Detailing Shots 28
    Drinks in Turn.. 30
    Emotional Opposites 32
    Equipment Envy.. 34
    Excessive Celebration 36
    Faking Poor Fundamentals 38
    "Friendly" Insults 40
    Gayness 42
    Generation Gap... 44
    Health Queries.. 46
    Helpfulness 48
    How & Why 50
    Ignoring 52
    Injuries 54
    Invisible Friend 56
    Jokes 58
    Jump Starting.. 60
    Late to Begin... 62
    Lingering 64
    Listening... 66
    Lucky Me 68
    Medical Cane... 70
    Missing Ball 72
    Musical Auditions 74
    Nervous Enhancement 76
    Nit Picking 78
    Noises... 80
    Odd Habits... 82
    Old Geezer... 84
    Partner Divorce... 86

Personal Tragedy 88
Politics 90
Powder & Chalk 92
Practical Joker 94
Propositions 96
Put-downs 98
Rules Expert.. 100
Self-inflicted Delusions 102
Self-doubt... 104
Sex Appeal.. 106
Shark Yourself 108
Shockers 110
Slow Racker 112
Slow Shooter... 114
Smoking... 116
Stand By Me.. 118
Stick Whisperer 120
Storyteller 122
Sympathy... 124
Table Critic Advisor... 126
Team Tricks 128
Temper Tantrum 130
Thinker 132
Time-outs.. 134
Waiting to play 136
Waive the Penalty 138
MINOR SHARKS.. 140
Advance Notice... 141
Am I in your way? 142
Annoyances 143
Concession.. 146
Fake 8 Ball Handicap 147
Leading Questions... 148
My Stick is Better.. 149
Nagger... 150
Overused Words 151
Self Talker 152
Start and Stop 153
The Gang is All Here 154
Waffler... 155
SOME FINAL WORDS... 156
About Hustlers & Sharking 156
How Hustlers Research Victims 158
BY THE SAME AUTHOR 160
ACKNOWLEDGEMENTS.. 161

Welcome

Random House Dictionary definitions:

competition - *rivalry between two or more persons or groups for an object desired in common, usually resulting in a victor and a loser.*

gamesmanship *(aka "hustling") - 1. the use of methods, esp. in a sports contest, that are dubious or seemingly improper but not strictly illegal. 2. the technique or practice of manipulating people or events so as to gain an advantage or outwit one's opponents or competitors.*

shark *- 1. (v) to obtain by trickery. 2. (n) a person regarded as ruthless.* ***(added)*** *3. (n) any pool player who wins*

++

The concept of friendly gamesmanship (sharking) was first documented in Stephen Potter's book (written in 1947), *The Theory and Practice of Gamesmanship, or How to Win without Really Cheating*. This humorous sports book identified the many common tricks used by sportsman of the day to win by helping others lose.

Nowadays, the gentle limits of sportsmanship no longer seem to apply. You, as a pool player, must educate yourself on the many sharks used in pool halls, bars, and home game rooms.

This book provides the tools and tips needed to recognize these mind games - and thereby avoid being a victim of pool sharks and hustlers. However fiercely you may cling to the high ideals of upstanding sportsmanship, the reality of the world is that hustling and sharking is everywhere.

RECOMMENDATION: The author suggests this material be used to protect yourself – with this one exception:

IF someone attempts to use any of these sharks against you – that person has given tacit permission to use this entire library. Under that condition, have fun.

How Sharking Works

Sharking is designed to bend or break an opponent's concentration and ability to focus on the game. These and thousands of other tricks have been around a long time. It is so pervasive in the world that Sun Tzu incorporated it in his "The Art of War", and that was written 2,500 years ago.

If you do a close study of newspaper accounts of the great billiards and pool championships played in the 1800's, there were plenty of accusations and counter-accusations of distractive tricks.

Sharking can be as obvious as the famous pocket coin-jingling trick while standing close to your opponent's blind side. It can be so subtle that you may not even realize the shark occurred until after the money has been paid out. What you thought were merely little habits of your opponent could very easily be intentional destroyers of your playing concentration.

On the other hand, you can spend too much time considering what actions and words by your opponent are intended distractions. You could get to the point where someone saying "hello" is a shark (who knows, it might be). Paranoia may be one of the great unknown health risks of playing cue sports.

Most of the time, you get common wanna-be hustlers who apply the most crass, low-class, and obviously stupid tricks. It is possible that someone used those juvenile tricks on them and they fell for it. Therefore, in their opinion, that particular shark should work on every other pool player in the world. Fortunately, with knowledge gained from this book, these players are easily re-sharked, and they are quickly turned into victims of your counter-efforts.

Be aware that some players see sharking as an art form and a necessary competitive skill. These experienced hustlers apply each maneuver as part of a strategic program, each designed to help them win games and matches. All they want is to take the money.

Experienced pool hustlers have a very large library of tricks, ready to be adapted to any competitor's personality and playing style. Rather than a sledge hammer approach of the amateur hustlers, they prefer the gentle taps of a carefully placed psychological chisel against your psyche.

Once you recognize what is happening, the correct reaction is to take intelligent action against the pool fool. DO NOT "EVER" get upset or angry. That reduction in your focus and concentration is exactly what he wants to accomplish.

The material in this book provides all the necessary tools to not only turn the tables, but also to significantly improve your winning opportunities.

Life Examples of Sharking

In the real world (the rest of the planet outside of the pool room), consider these examples.

- A girlfriend, with a simple smile and wistful, appealing little-girl look easily drags you through the mall, store by store, by your nose. She knows how to shark.

- Your sister's kid throws a temper tantrum when you say "No" – and you pretty much always give in. Hustled by a kid - tsk, tsk.

- Your Mom says, "People are starving in Africa." You reluctantly force the boiled cabbage (or beets, or carrots) down our throat. She gamed you! (And don't try the "Let's send it to them.") By the way, all mothers are master gamesmanship tricksters and child manipulators.

The common element in all sharks is that your intention was to do one thing, and somehow you ended up doing something else. These mind games are designed to push you in someone else's preferred direction, regardless of any original intentions and plans.

By the way, skillful and knowledgeable pool playing, or a lucky roll is NOT sharking. It really is bad sportsmanship and poor manners to accuse anyone of sharking when they are simply better players.

Note: No scientific study has ever been done to determine just how common sharking is, in relationships, family, friendships, various sports, etc. It might be worth a Ph.D. to some enterprising college kid.

Major Sharks

These are the efforts (listed alphabetically) commonly used by pool players of all skills and all over the planet. There are many variations of these. Take your time and study these tricks. This knowledge makes your competitive life less complicated. Regardless whether the attempted performance is from an amateur wannabe or experienced pool gamesman, knowledge is the key.

Some people use sharks unconsciously. Some will be friends who want to mess with your mind to win a "friendly game". There are also real pool hustlers. These guys do not miss a trick in modifying their odds of winning. Educate yourself with the material in this book.

Accusations

Here is how the pool hustler applies this shark. Any "apparent" excuse attacking your sportsmanship works. For example, on a break shot that you racked, the balls don't spread very well. In an angry tone, he accuses you of improper racking. What you don't know is that he took some speed off the break shot. This keeps the balls clustered so that the table layout validates his accusations of your intentional cheating.

You might think his attack is some sort of poor joke – or you got stuck playing someone with a bad temper. After a second or third accusation, you will begin to get irritated at his besmirching your good name.

But this is merely the beginning. At every opportunity, he finds some reason to accuse you of poor sportsmanship, cheating, and then lying about cheating. Some will be irritating comments; one or two will include a raised voice.

He wants to play against an irritated and frustrated opponent. He will carefully analyze your state of mind. If it appears that you are beginning to restore a calm, analytical attitude, he will throw out the needed comments and declarations that will keep you from performing well.

4

If you are not reactive enough, he can increase the volume and intensity. For example, coming up to the table and stares down at your shot. If you ask him to back off, he refuses, saying, "I'm making sure you don't cheat."

Response

Actually, you have many options to "manage" this type of shark. If you are an aggressive competitor with some acting ability, use the direct, but louder counter-attack. With greater emphasis, accuse him of being the swindler and scammer. Make sure you don't push into his personal space, which could start a fist fight. Instead, make your declamations from the other side of the table. What you want is for others to come to the rescue. He can be set back on his heels for a short time, so concentrate on winning the next few games as quickly as possible.

You can take the "reactionary" approach, which requires less acting skill. Pretend to have a nervous breakdown. Perform a semi-collapse near the table. Declare that you have a heart condition and can't possibly get upset or you could die. Ask him if he is trying to kill you. Play this performance to the audience. Solicit their sympathy and support. (Extra point if he apologizes.)

Here is the low road approach. Declare to everyone, "Guilty and proud of it" approach. Respond with a sneer and a challenge, such as, "Yeah, I'm sharking you. What are you going to do about it?" Every time he misses a shot, you call out, "Sharked you - again." By the time the match is over, his sanity becomes questionable. Be a little careful with this, he could become violent.

Here is a high road response. Demand (with intensity), "Prove it. Explain what I did to shark or cheat you." Stand your ground and ask for proof. If available, drag in any railbirds to be your jury and request a judgment from them.

Alzheimer's

This is an old geezer shark - usually pulled on young players by a mid-fifties or older old guy. It's usually done more to yank the younger shooter's chain then for serious hustling. If you see this scheme in action, stay and watch the match. It can be quite entertaining.

The old fella, with all due seriousness, constantly asks his opponent which ball he should be shooting. Occasionally, he stands stock still for a long time while it is still his turn. He only moves when reminded to shoot. He says in surprise, "It's my turn? Are you sure?" This is alternated with complaints about problems with old age.

For example, in an 8 ball game, on every other shot he turns to his competitor and asks, "Am I stripes or solids?" In 9 Ball, he queries, "Which one is next?" When it is his turn, he stays in his chair, intently watching the table. After about 15 seconds, he looks over to the youngster and says, "Why aren't you shooting? It's your turn, isn't it?"

The old fellow accomplishes several things all at the same time. He forces his opponent's attention from the game and the necessary thinking needed for proper tactics. He wants to build up a level of frustration. At the same time, the old guy wants to make the youngster reach an assumption that the old guy just can't be a serious competitor.

The old geezer further covers up his skills with a blanket of confusion. He randomly stops at any point in the game to turn away from the table to say hello to a passing acquaintance. He gets down on a shot, does a couple practice strokes, then suddenly rises and asks if it is still his turn.

He may even ask confusing questions, and then ignore any answers. With this buffoon-like facade, his young competitor doesn't quite realize how carefully the old man is playing each shot. Nothing fancy, but all resulting in situations to the oldster's advantage and the youngster's disadvantage.

All of this work is designed to dull his opponent's thinking, as well as hide his own sensible shooting selections. This trick can overcome a significant skill difference.

Response

When you see it applied to younger players, don't interfere. All young people need life lessons. It part of the process of becoming a seasoned adult (as well as a competent player). Being exposed to an oldster who wins with cunning tricks is one of those necessary experiences. After all, some day they too will be able to use this shark on upcoming youngsters.

Watching this happen is always worth the time - and you might pick up a trick or two for later use. If anyone is interested in side bets, put a few bucks on the old fellow.

If you are this guy's opponent, the best response to this shark is to concentrate on playing your game. Don't allow his random statements to affect your competitive focus. Treat him as you would any other competitive shooter.

As an alternative, you can use a more proactive approach. As he is making his declarations of confusion, be more "helpful". Start anticipating his queries by pointing out which ball he should shoot next.

You can even recommend how the shot should be played and which ball should be the next target. Not only can you be generous with your advice, you can even go to the table to assist him in setting up for a shot. Come up close and check his line of aim and stance. Offer suggestions to improve.

Another option is to give him a nickname. Start calling him Old Dude or Gramps – as in, "Hey Gramps. Take the 3 ball next." "Come on Gramps. You can do better than that." etc.

Eventually, he will realize this trick isn't working and the game should settle out to a match focusing on skill. This is not to say that he won't apply another mind game – but generally, being "found out" is enough to make him behave for the rest of the match. He's had his fun.

Back & Forth

On this sharking effort, the pool hustler wants to interrupt the game flow and rhythm. He does this by continuously moving from the table to his equipment and burning up groups of seconds and minutes. These back-and-forth movements are only done during his turn at the table.

The amount of time he uses up almost forces your attention onto him instead of the table. The timing of this shark can be continuous throughout the match, or only applied during critical parts of each game. If not recognized as a trick, this can do a lot of damage to your will to win.

If there is a coin toss to determine who gets the first shot at scoring, he interrupts, saying, "I've got something that's cool." He goes back to his equipment, digs around a bit (30 seconds or so), and then pulls out an unusual coin. "Let's use this lucky coin. It's always lucky for one of us." After the toss, he picks it up, returns the coin to its storage - another small delay of 20-30 seconds.

When it is his turn, he gets up from his chair, comes slowly to the table, and looks like he's thinking about tactics. Suddenly, he says something like, "Oops, forgot something." He strides back to his stuff, digs around (more delay), comes up with something. Fiddles with it (more delay), and then comes back to the table. Of course, play can only resume upon his "schedule".

Another variation is to do a couple practice strokes, and then jump up to get his special (or favorite, or lucky) chalk for his stick. Of course, this requires another trip – and time to find. More seconds pass by as he diligently chalks the cue tip. After careful inspection and a few touchups, he restores the chalk to his bag and (finally) returns to the table. As if this weren't enough, he acts as if the interruption made him forget the tactical plan – and he begins his table analysis all over again.

Individually, these interruptions are not distractive or immediately affect your focus and concentration. But cumulatively, it takes a toll on your patience and tolerance. This trick does not affect the early part of the match, or even the middle set of games. It is designed to be a major distractive factor during the critical end games in the match.

Response

If you are a very patient person, amuse yourself by watching his antics and efforts to seem believable. Keep in mind that his performance of these activities requires a certain amount of physical and mental effort. And there is an excellent chance, that by simply doing nothing, your patience outruns his acting abilities.

When he begins one of these dances, the time can be well-used for your benefit. Take this time to evaluate the table layout and consider some of the dozens of shooting options, both offensive and defensive. This mental exercise allows you to do some calculations on lesser options. Calculate the cue ball speed and spin. Consider the opportunities of follow versus draw. This can become an excellent opportunity to train your mind to consider multiple tactical shots.

If you are somewhat less patient and want to take a more active role, here are a couple of options:

• Wait for him to "forget" something. When he picks up the object, walk over to him and start asking questions. You can come up with quite a few questions, such as, "What is that?", "How much did you pay?", "Where can I get one like that?" "Is really any good?" Using these why, what, where, and how questions significantly distract his own concentration on the game.

• When you notice him going to his equipment, step in front of him. Accidently force him to walk around you. Repeat on the return trip. Apologize profusely on any of his complaints, but continue to get in his way.

Do NOT, I repeat, do NOT get emotional or show any negative reaction. That is why he is doing this shark. Since he wants to distract your attention, when you intrude on his little delaying activities, you can throw off his routines.

Bad Shot Commentary

All players have situations where a shot or scoring attempt was missed, or the layout of the table is less than ideal for the next attempt. This is part of the ups and downs of competitive play.

This becomes a sharking trick when your opponent makes one or more comments on your failures. These are freely offered on any poor consequence or where the playing situation is less than ideal for advancement.

There can be many reasons for the balls on the table not being where you wanted them to end up. Your failure of intent might be caused by a badly misjudged shot selection, maybe a poor tactical choice, or simply the result of not thinking what could happen.

It is when you are just realizing your lack of success that the hustler inserts his snarky comments. This is usually presented in a joking manner and without any apologies for his barely suppressed happiness over your bad luck.

Here are some of the more common comments he can use to make you feel worse:

- "That's a bit of bad luck."
- "Could you have done any worse?"
- "That was terrible."
- "What an unlucky roll."
- "That almost came out perfect."
- "You needed just a little more (or less) speed on that shot."
- "You should have been more accurate."
- "So close, so far away."
- "You must have really pissed off the sporting gods."
- "I bet you wish you could shoot that over."
- "That could have had a better result."
- "Are you really that bad?"
- "I can show you how to shoot that correctly."

When you begin your inning with a less than ideal table layout, here are a few comments he offers:

- "That's a tough position to start in."
- "I don't see anything that you can do with this."
- "That's not quite the worst spot to start from."
- "Tsk, tsk, tsk." with sad, slow shaking of the head.

All of these are not welcome. But it is his attitude that takes the joy out of playing against him. He enjoys your lack of success with unabashed pleasure.

Response

The worst action you can take when suffering this constant denigration of your shooting skills is to get pissed off and start beating him up. Below are better solutions. However, if for some reason the guy just can't be brought under control – make sure you have the approval of railbirds to begin the more physical actions to restrict his verbiage. (Some might even help out.)

When the hustler starts using this distractive effort on you, your first attempt should be done with a straight-forward request. Make an offer something like, "Let's make an agreement. If you don't say anything about my game, I won't say anything about yours. Deal or not?"

If he agrees, you've stopped this specific sharking trick. (Be warned, that if he considers himself to be a master gamesman, he has more sharks ready to use.) BUT, if he doesn't agree with all due seriousness, he has given you permission to offer the same commentary on his "problems".

Here is a passive-resistive approach. When your turn comes up, do not immediately go up to the table. Just wait until he informs you about your turn. On the first comment he makes, start disassembling your stick and get ready to leave. While he is open-mouthed at this action – don't forget to grab any betting funds. On any questions, say, "I don't play with idiots. Let me know when you stop being stupid." If you scarfed up some money, say, "in the meantime, I'm taking this as your penalty."

Bellyacher

Life can be a bowl of cherries or it can be the pits. Any opponent who uses this has chosen the low road and decided to be that bowl of pits. His efforts also put him at the top of your "DO NOT be friends with ..." list.

This is rarely an intentional shark. The guy's life might actually be so bad he can't stop himself from complaining. Regardless of intention, this makes the playing atmosphere toxic to your concentration. At least one good thing – no master hustler would attempt this type of shark, simply because the acting would also affect his game skills.

This opponent starts the match by complaining – about something, doesn't matter what. When he isn't complaining about one thing, he's whining about another. Just saying hello is enough to get him going.

His every statement offers only a negative viewpoint. He has personal problems and intends to make you very aware of them. No matter how hard you try to fade into the background, you have, unfortunately, become his audience of choice.

This is probably the guy's natural attitude. He's certainly not someone you want to regularly compete against. If you started the match with expectations of enjoying yourself, by mid-match, you do not.

His continuous negativity burns away any enthusiasm you had at the beginning of the game. His careless shooting affects your careful concentration. To sum it up, this individual actually deserves the problems, bad luck, and limited opportunities he's complaining about. His suffering is a self-fulfilling prophecy.

If his negative verbosity is from his heart, his bellyaching is not a disguise to hide his skills. He is not attempting to trick you into playing worse than you really are. He is actually feeling and demonstrating his normal personality. You just happen to be the nearest trapped target of his attention.

Anyone carrying this amount of negative emotions rarely offers a competitive challenge. Even though he isn't making a serious attempt at winning, you are still being distracted.

Response

The passive approach would be to hunker down, turn off your ears, and do your best to ignore his words and attitude. This requires an intense effort to maintain enough focus and concentration to win quickly.

Alternately, you can turn your feelings of irritation into a powerful drive to win. Use the internal thought of "How dare this bastard try to ruin my fun?" as an incentive.

Cut back on your shooting expectations. When any shot is difficult, play defensively so that he does not have a good shot when he starts his turn. This ensures that at best, he only gets one shot before sitting down. The quicker you can beat him, the quicker you can get away from his presence.

There is one approach that might help take some pressure off your brain. Take the role of agreeing with whatever he says. Use the supporting "I think you are completely right." "Tell me more." The deeper he is buried in his world of woe, the quicker you can get to the win.

If this is too much bother, go with the traditional process perfected by husbands who don't want to pay too much attention to their wife's talking. The agreeable "Uh huh.", "OK.", and "Mmmm." should work enough to allow you to ignore his commentaries. This puts his conversations into the background – similar to the way you handle bad jukebox music. You get to ignore him as you work on beating him as quickly as possible. It's not like you are going to be tested on the content of his conversations.

Bigmouth

To be effective with this distraction, the pool hustler has to be part entertainer, part narrator, part master of ceremonies, and full-time conversational hog. He must have a personality style that demands to be the center of everyone's attention.

Probably the most memorable person who made this a centerpiece of his entire professional lifestyle is Rudolf Wanderone, also known as Minnesota Fats. He was recognized as one of the most well-known hustlers of pool in the USA in the 1940's, 1950's, and 1960's. He was so entertaining that he became a television star on his sheer talent to talk while playing. Without apologies, he was an almost unstoppable force, keeping a shrewd mind hidden behind a constant stream of fascinating and humorous comments, stories, and observations. The very flow of his words overwhelmed the majority of his competitors both on the table and off.

Whether playing or not, your opponent keeps up a pattern. Any conversational contributions you attempt to make are immediately steam-rollered. He knows what he is doing and the affect it has on people. The rapid-fire verbiage almost forces a requirement to pay attention to his word flow. And of course, this achieves his purpose – to significantly reduce your concentration on the game as well as interfering with the necessary game analysis.

Questions are asked, rapid-fire style. Respond quickly, because he won't leave you much time to answer. It goes something like, "So when did you first start playing?" If you don't say something quickly, he answers his own question. "You were probably about 13, right?" That initiates a recounting of some adventure he had at that age.

If you happen to come into the presence of a true master of this shark, sit in the background and watch the show. It is theater that you cannot buy a ticket to get into. Do not play for money against him, but a side bet on his success probably pays off. Watch and enjoy as he takes apart any opponent. It should be one of the better entertainment experiences of your life.

Response

When this type of hustler becomes your match opponent, there are a few things you need to do. First and most important, do not attempt to go word for word with him.

He has years of experience in separating his game playing skills from his mouth. Instead, remove yourself as his primary audience. One response would be to do some fake snoozing while he is shooting and talking. You might be surprised how well closing your eyes helps you keep control of your mental attitude. The relaxation and even breathing pattern can help you experience almost zen-like benefits.

Alternately, you can engage in conversation with a nearby railbird. Be sure to face your discussion partner so that your opponent is completely out of sight. Your effort of ignoring his attempts to be the center of your attention helps slow him down.

When his questions are not related to the game or match, use a wave of your hand (a sign of "don't bother me") as you intently stare at the table. Essentially, by bobbing and weaving your attention, you can keep away from the full force of his verbiage.

While it takes some effort to do this, it is less damaging to your concentration than having to directly fend off his verbal assaults. This helps limit the distractive damage.

If you want to try a personal request to stop, make it during the first few minutes of the match. Whether he honors that request is debatable. And even if he agrees, you have to be careful that he doesn't start nibbling around the edges of the agreement.

Be vigilant and enforce any "quiet" agreement immediately on the first utterances he might make. Do this by stopping any playing activity, fully face him and bring your index finger up to your pursed lips for the traditional "be quiet" signal.

Boring

Are you an individual who is courteous and attentive to others when they talk? Do you try your best to "get along"? If you fit this profile, you might find yourself the victim of this trap.

To make this work, the pool hustler uses a double step-down approach intended to dull your keen competitive edge. When the match starts, he needs to convince you, either by attitude or by his shooting, that he is unconcerned about winning this match.

Once you start emulating his laid-back playing attitude, the next step is to maintain your lack of concern. He uses phrases like, "It's not important who wins. It's only important to have fun." Comments like these can easily cause you to relax your focus and competitive intent. After all, he's not trying to be competitive, so why should you?

Even if you resist his call to be lazy and kick back to enjoy a relaxing round with a friend, he continues to persuade you of the relative unimportance of this competition.

Once your intense desire to battle for ascendancy is squashed, he applies the second level of this trap. Once you stepped down your competitive intensity, he has to make sure that you stay non-competitive.

He now becomes the "talker", not for the purpose of entertainment, but to keep you lulled and relaxed. The subjects he brings up are non-controversial and boring (hence the name of this shark). Nothing he says is designed to involve your interest or attention.

He rambles on about material that simply doesn't require you to pay attention. His tone is monotone – delivered flatly and without emphasis. For example, something like:

- My high school invited me to a reunion. I think it was the 15th, or maybe 10th – I can't remember. <ramble, ramble, ramble>.

- I read a book about moss the other day. It talked about 20 major species and about 200 varieties. There was this black moss that <ramble, ramble, ramble>

The monotone sound of his voice slowly develops a slightly numbing effect on your mind. And that's all he needs to accomplish.

He plays to fit this approach. There is no single-inning runout, no dramatic three-rail banks, nothing to call attention to his true table skills.

He just consistently plays a little better than you do. When you come to the table, you have something to shot – it just won't be easy. Because you are not playing seriously, your chances of missing increase significantly.

When he wins, he apologizes. You even win a few games – just not enough to get ahead. Basically, he just barely keeps ahead of you.

Some players who use this shark are doing so not because of an evil heart. Through trial and error over months and even years, they discovered this tactic to prevent intense competition. This has become a mechanism to make competitors match their dulled down emotions.

Response

The problem with recognizing this shark is recognizing this shark. An entire match can be lost before you realize what is going on. Therefore, your first and best protection from this trick is the strength of your focus and attention. This is one of the few situations where you want to have fun playing the table and not the opponent. Treating every shot as a puzzle to solve very effectively offsets your opponent's efforts.

Another response that helps is to assign his rambling to the level of background noise. Use automated acknowledgements (grunts and hrumphs) to disconnect your attention to anything he says.

There is one proactive response. In the process of his dull communications, ask follow-up questions related to his topic. Express and interest in the topic. This interrupts his placid playing attitude and affects his ability to focus. You interaction splits his attention between answering your questions and playing the table. He ends up distracting himself.

Cell Phone

If you are one of those individuals who absolutely must stay in instant contact with everyone in the world, via your smart phone and other devices, you are an easy victim of this distraction. Your obsession with communications (voice, text, email, chat etc.) with friends and non-pool players is a destructive habit in any competitive situation. Just when you need to focus and concentrate on a critical win/lose effort, receiving a phone call or text message is guaranteed to disrupt your competitive spirit.

The smart phone (and other communication devices) offers an insidious freedom to anyone else on the planet to intrude on your life. These robbers who steal minutes of your existence are able to do so, with a simple press of a button or two. There is nothing you can do to prevent them from reaching out to you. With the wide proliferation of these devices, you can never know how far your phone number has traveled.

A tech-savvy pool hustler only needs to notice that you are sensitive to phone ringing – your own or anyone else's phone. When a phone rings, he pays close attention to your face. If you look towards the ring of someone else's phone, or if you automatically make a move to take your phone out – he knows you can be sharked.

When your phone rings while playing:

1. Any current game thinking processes stop. This includes table analysis and tactical considerations.

2. Any physical actions stop. If down on the shot, the execution is stopped.

3. You have to pick up and look at the phone to identify who is calling.

Whether you answer or not is immaterial. The shark has already worked. When you bring your attention back to the table, everything must begin again.

The entire table analysis must be restarted. Shooting options must be reconsidered. If you had the glimmerings of a clever shot, the idea probably is completely forgotten, lost in the world of "could have been".

To implement this dastardly plan, the pool hustler can have a nearby buddy make the call, by simply giving any kind of signal. The timing is selected for maximum disruption of your game. If you do answer, because you are curious by the unknown number, here are some possible "excuses":

- "Sorry, I dialed the wrong number."

- Fake sales call, "Do you need new pots & pans? I have a deal for you."

- Fake spam pitch, "Do you want a joke a day? Call 555-5555 and hang up."

- Even a text message can work, i.e., "Hey, pick up pizza."

There is a variation of this shark. If your phone number has been properly shielded from public knowledge, the buddy conspirator calls the pool hustler's phone. That phone is pre-configured loud and irritating ring tone for an incoming call, or something equally messy for an incoming text.

The call can be ignored – as long as you have reacted to the noise. Alternately, the call can be picked up. A loud fake conversation can take place. An argumentative tone is very effective, since he can "lose his temper" as an excuse to raise his voice.

Response

Table billiards is a sport where intrusive communication devices are very unwelcome. Anytime you play pool, turn off or otherwise silence any and all phones, pagers, tablets, etc. If you are obsessively interested in communicating with anyone who wants a slice of your life – check the phone between games or give it to a friend to monitor for important calls/messages.

If your opponent is using his phone to affect your concentration, stop playing and sit down. Inform him you are not moving until he turns off his device. Stick to your guns on this requirement.

Clothes & Accessories

There are a few pool hustlers who use this shark very effectively. The use of clothing and accessories can be very distractive. The variety of choices and options is extensive. The cost to outfit for this distraction does not have to be expensive. Many second-hand stores, thrift shops, charity outlets, etc. can provide a wide variety of unusual wearable articles.

There are multiple levels in which this shark can affect your game. The outfit could be visually clashing with wild colors. It could by stylistically classing (i.e., actual or almost costume-like). If you are a clothes horse, he can engender incitement of envy with obviously cool items (i.e., a perfectly tailored outfit, or <any animal>skin boots, hats, etc.)

When visually distractive, just his movement anywhere in your line of sight can affect your concentration.

The pool hustler does not intend to hide his candle under a bushel. He wants to be noticeable from anywhere in a big room. Just his walking around draws all eyes to his attire.

Clothes and accessories can be theme-based. They can be historical from various time periods and eras. He could be the fancy dress of 1850's European gentry, a zoot suit throw-back to the 1940s, the cowboy of the 1880s, or the Victorian gentleman.

Dress themes can be ethnic-based, such as African chic or Hawaiian beach. You might even see a rhinestone cowboy (urban version) with fancy embroidery and colorful glitter. The guy might simply intend a violently clash of colors – no theme intended.

Further eye interference can be incorporated through the inclusion of assorted accessories. These can be any variety of items from a clashing silk scarf or a fancy pure-white sash with gold buttons. Other articles of distraction could any variety of hats, belts, ties, vests, head bands, etc.

Bling (all fake of course) can be overdone for a huge visual distraction. This can include everything from wrist bands, arm bands, necklaces, and head bands.

This shark is not just intended to affect your visual and style senses. He can also extend its distractive value by infecting your mind with useless information. At various opportunities, he expounds on details about his clothing and accessory choices. This can include nonsensical historical background, the discovery and purchase background, and on, and on.

He could further engage your attention by finding fault with your clothing choices. Even if you refuse to participate in conversation, he does so with railbirds, while you are shooting.

Response

There are several effective tactics. If he is verbose, before the match begins, compliment him on individual items. Ask about where and when it came into his possession, and how much.

Keep asking questions and make him react to your efforts. Continue requesting more details and information throughout the match. At the very least, he has a problem assembling an effective table strategy. When you notice he starts avoiding eye contact, you own him.

Another tactical option is to express your distaste for shallow individuals who are soooo much more interested in themselves instead of caring for the problems being inflicted on the weak and helpless of the world. Used aggressively to overrun his attempts to change the conversation, you can force him to huddle in a corner.

Another tactic, especially useful when he obviously loves the sound of his voice, is the "silent stand and stare" technique. When you get up for your turn at the table, face him directly and stare at him. Eventually, this gets his attention. When he finally asks, "What?" say something similar to, "Shut up when I am shooting." He may have a short-term memory problem, so this may need to be repeated. Even the most oblivious person gets the message after five or six repetitions.

And, as a last resort, this trick reduces his ability to concentrate on shooting. Just as he is getting up for his shot, give him a compliment about an accessory or something. Doing this just before he shoots effectively steals his concentration.

Compliments

This is an insidious effort, and one of the easiest sharking tricks that a pool hustler can implement. His compliments on various aspects of your pool game are delivered with obvious sincerity and clothed in good sportsmanship. This shark is successful when you react with touchy-feely enhancements to your self-esteem.

In pool, as well as other life activities, anytime you start thinking highly of yourself, there is a leveling force (call it the universal teeter-tooter) that applies reality to your fantasies. These attitude adjustments are brutal. The more you think you got the goods, the harder the slap-down.

To quote the Bible, King James Version, Proverbs 16:18 "Pride goeth before destruction, and a haughty spirit before a fall." When you accept your opponent's flattery as the truth, the whole truth, and nothing but the truth – there is a significant degradation of your competitive attitude.

The first couple failures might not affect your assumptions, but third poorly considered shot starts a leak in your inflated ego. IN the meantime, he picks up a couple of easy wins.

He constantly closely watches your reactions. When he starts on the bright sincere-like approach, any facial response to the flattery encourages him. When you include a "Thank you", he knows and owns you.

So, let's say you are a superior competitor. No fair words or sweet compliments can sway your rugged determination to play each shot with dedicated serious intent.

The pool hustler simply turns this compliment shark from the sweetness and light approach to the dark side. With simple adjustments in tone, he can take the same complimentary words and apply a vicious edge. Instead of trying to butter you up, he hands you compliments that do not deserve even the most minor recognition.

On the simplest and easiest of shots, he expresses praise with obvious banality. Even shots worthy or real respect are dissed with the same bland "good shot" verbiage.

22

This starts out with simplistic standard two word phrases – "Good shot." "Not bad." etc. Then, as the mid-match games are played, additional commentary is included - such as, "You must have worked pretty hard to master that type of shot."

Other commentary can include statements like, "You're a pretty good shooter." and "That was excellent control." and "I've seen a lot of shooters. You're on your way to becoming one of the better players." All of these are delivered in a monotone, devoid of good intent.

The "irritating" version of this shark also introduces "Good try." And "You almost got it." on misses and poor shape for the next shot. This, of course, just adds insult to injury. Not only are you frustrated on the failure, he is stating the obvious.

Response

If you are able to relegate his commentary to background noise, nothing he says, on the bright or dark side of compliments affects your game. You essentially play the table with a deaf ear.

If you tend to be "sensitive" to actions and sounds around you, there are ways to deflect his efforts. Take his attempts and go proactive. Apply this same shark on his shots – but with greater emphasis and obvious insincerity.

Instead of the simplistic two word phrases ("Good shot."), expand with additional adjectives/adverbs, i.e., "REALLY good shot." Etc. If you wish, you can throw in a sentence or two of how the shot was so amazing and fantastic – you get the idea. Continue doing this until you feel some sense of physical danger.

At this point, play the bigger and better man, and offer a truce. Negotiate a deal for both of you to cease and desist, so that the game can move on. That should end it.

However, if the guy is (or thinks he is) a master hustler, he abides by the one agreement – and simply move on to another of his bag of tricks. Constant vigilance against known hustlers is necessary.

Consoling

Somewhere, someplace, maybe in an alternate universe, there is a book entitled "The Correct Behavior of Bad Sportsmanship". If there was such a book, there would be a section that talks about proper behavior of a player when his competitor suffers a massive reversal of fortune. In that section would be recommendations for proper decorum of competitors, spectators, and friends. These gamesmanship responses to the player's tragedy would range from unsympathetic observations to expressions of heartfelt sorrow for the poor suffering victim.

This little sharking distraction would be fully detailed and documented in that section. This tactic is applied against you immediately after some sort of major pool table disaster. The effort to console you would be of such magnitude that it totally disintegrates your concentration for many innings.

In 9 ball, it would be offered up after a perfect and precise run of the first 8 balls, with an easy duck sitting 4 inches from the corner pocket. Confidently getting down on the shot, you setup and make the stroke – arise to the expected cheers of your supporters only to hear a massive groan fill the room. Also missing is the expected plop of the ball into the pocket. You instantly know you face a table disaster. And, as expected, there is the 9 ball resting on the edge of the pocket.

<Pause for you the reader to fully imagine the situation.>

This is when your opponent starts applying the Consoling shark and wastes no time in getting started. For the pool hustler, there are multiple benefits. First, he takes the knife in your heart and starts twisting it. Then he gets to extend your suffering over several games. All of these little kindly presented but vicious efforts are designed to throw your game off – helping him win the match and take his rewards.

Watching your face and reactions carefully, he begins the mental destruction of your will to win. With a sorrowful tone of voice, he pats your back, and says something like one of the following:

- "Don't worry. You can do better. I have faith in you."

- "That could have happened to anyone."

- "I wish there was a Do-Over rule."

This is intended to remind you of your disaster which in turn delays your mental recovery and extends the time you apply personal self-castigation. While you are focused on your drastic failure as a pool player, you have little ability to play well. And, if you do start putting the experience behind you, your opponent cautions you to be careful so that a similar mistake is not made. He even wishes you good luck on a critical shot.

Response

Most important - stifle your immediate reaction to turn around and punch him heavily in the bread basket. If you were to follow your impulses, you would be in police custody very quickly. Instead, use all of your self-restraint and put on your best poker face. Ignore him and don't acknowledge any communication from him.

Do not immediately resume play after a major setback. Take a break or a time out to recover your emotional equilibrium and mental balance. Get away from the playing area and perform a few physical exercises such as deep knee bends, a round of quick toe-touches, or a couple minutes of jogging in place. This burns off some of the emotional energy you are trying to keep under control.

Let the physical effort wash away the tense after-effects of the bad experience. Then do some deep breathing to fill your body with oxygen. Be careful to avoid hyper-ventilation.

Then, with your emotions back under control, and your brain ready to get back into the action, return and do your best with renewed intentions to win. You have a chance to recover if you can regain and maintain concentration on the shot at hand. You do not have a chance if you go temporarily insane.

Whenever your opponent attempts to shark you with this trick – smile. Say, "Thank you. This match isn't over until it's over." Gird your loins with fierce determination and get back into the game.

Cripple Yourself

This shark tricks you into playing well below your regular speed. It's designed to weaken your intention to win by demonstrating a huge difference is skills between you and your opponent. After all, the guy obviously doesn't have the skills to be a serious competitor.

During the first couple of games, usually with very small bets (for the fun of it), your opponent demonstrates this difference in skills. When this is obvious, he begins saying things like:

"I can't possibly have any chance of winning against you. You are just too good." Follow-up complaints can include, "Why are you playing so hard against me. I'm not that good of a player. Aren't we playing for fun?"

These communications are designed to shame you into not taking the games seriously. Once you start "accepting" these requests to back off on your competitive spirit, it is very easy to relax your standards and just start banging off shots without thought or consideration of the table consequences.

When he is successful in modifying your playing attitude, you start committing a number of pool playing sins. Because the competition becomes less important, you spend less time and effort in table analysis. You also don't take enough time to properly calculate the shots, including aiming, along with the proper cue ball speed and spin. You intentionally downgrade your own skills, just to make your adversary feel better.

Now he can start to win a game here and there – all the while crying about the need for more fairness – when you win. Eventually, your playing intensity is dialed down so much that you become outright lazy. He has convinced you that the "value" of winning is unimportant. With no reason to focus and concentrate on the game, it becomes acceptable that your opponent starts winning more games. And, when he does win, the hustler apologizes while saying it was just pure accidental luck.

Relaxing playing standards also leads to the emergence of bad habits that you struggled hard to overcome. You don't get down the shot, you brain stops working, and even your stance starts getting sloppy. You stop considering defensive plays, completely. Basically, almost all of your fundamentals deteriorate.

In some cases, you don't even need your opponent to moan and groan or otherwise coerce you to downgrade your skills and abilities. You can easily become your own victim by intentionally hobbling yourself.

There is some research that indicates this impulse goes all the way back to when you were a toddler. The giants (adults) around you constantly badgered you into "sharing" toys and being nice. And when you didn't want to, punishment was quick to follow. In school, many teachers make it their life's goal to convince all of their students that the outcome of all games should be "fair" and "competition" is bad.

Response

There are times in life when making it all fair is an important and necessary action, especially when everyone is attempting to negotiate an equitable arrangement. Or, you might be playing with a bunch of buddies where the purpose is not to win games, but only to have a good time being together.

But in competition, this "fairness" impulse is a deadly sin and contributes to the loss of games what should never have occurred. Keep in mind this one most important fact: "There are no friends on the table." You can be friends before the match and you can be friends after the match, but not during the match.

The solution is actually quite simple – don't back off on your speed. If there is a real difference in skills (and the bets are relatively unimportant), handicap the games so that you must always play at your best. Some options are:

- If playing an absolute beginner, let him pick up the cue ball and position it for every shot.

- If playing someone with a few playing skills, but not a strong finisher - give him two turns for his inning.

- If there is a small disparity, give weight.

The main thing you want to ensure is something that forces you to play your best.

Detailing Shots

This shark is designed to slowly develop a strong sense of irritation and frustration. The pool hustler calls out every single ball action about every single shot - in excruciating detail.

This is not the regular information normally required in a call shot game. This is a full-blown and thoroughly complete description of the paths for every ball that he believes are to be moved by his shot. If that wasn't enough, he can make it worse. In the midst of this declaration of intent, he hesitates, re-thinks, and then explains redirections of one or more balls.

Everything is described from the initial cue tip/ball contact (speed/spin) until the table becomes a fresh still life. This can be presented as someone who wants to consider everything. It can also be explained in the tone of a professional lecture being given to total idiots (you).

Besides covering every possible table change, it also burns up large amounts of seconds. The considerable utterances of words keep you glued to your chair, while leaving him full freedom of movement around the table.

The process works something like this. First, he wanders around the table during his layout analysis, silently taking his time as he considers what he intends to do. Once he makes a decision, he begins self-explaining the patterns he has envisioned. Sometimes, about halfway through, an ad hoc ad-lib addition is included. The cue stick becomes a pointer to indicate expected results. He does this just loud enough for you to hear, but directed at himself as a verbal confirmation.

When he finally does get down to actually shoot, you are praying that he doesn't decide to rethink anything. It might help to send a prayer to the billiard gods. As you hold onto this fervent optimism, also add your sincere hope that he misses. If the object ball goes in, you are going to experience another episode of fantastical expectations.

Here is an example: "I'm going to shoot the 5 ball and make it hug the rail to the corner pocket (tracing the path with his stick). Since I want the cue ball to go over there (again using his stick), I'm going to hit the cue ball with 6:30 to come off the long rail in this direction, and then drift it over here (again tracing the path). I hope to miss these two balls (again pointing), and try to end up right there (putting the cue tip on the table to mark the spot)."

Be aware that there are a few individuals who do this unconsciously. That is simply their style of playing pool. If things didn't go as planned, he can be glib with the excuses. If you are an impatient individual, you can easily lose more games than you should.

Response

In the beginning of the competition, this shark won't be too distracting. As the match continues, it becomes more and more irritating. Fortunately, there are options.

One choice is to immediately start contributing to his statements. For example, as he describes the cue ball control and speed, chip in with, "Have you considered using a little left side spin draw instead? That helps you get here *<point with your stick>*. Plus, you can get better action off the rail."

Be sincere with your suggestions and recommendations. You can even come to the table and demonstrate your ideas on what goes where and how. When you proactively overlay his fantasies with your ideas, he becomes the reluctant recipient. If you can get him into an argument on who has the better plan – more power to you.

Another option is to stay in your chair. Become the doubter of his shooting decisions. For example, when he predicts a shot, call out, "I don't think it goes that way. I think that it goes to the head rail. You really want to reconsider your plan. It won't work."

If this is an intentional shark, these counter-sharks soon demonstrate that his trick is not working. The hustler abandons this effort and switch over to another. How smoothly he does this is dependent on his skill as a gamesman. If he's an amateur, it effectively shuts him up for the duration of the match.

Drinks in Turn

This is an old shark, commonly used back in the day when social activities were performed with polite and gracious courtesy. Within this environment, all competitive games demanded that opponents treat each other with the greatest level of good sportsmanship. This trick uses the social conventions surrounding the buying of drinks in turn between two players.

Drinks are defined here as alcoholic adult beverages. The purpose is to create a social obligation situation that is difficult for the victim to bring back into equilibrium. The affected individual becomes concerned because the perceived imbalance creates a nagging irritation. This mild frustration level is what reduces the effectiveness of your game. (In the social environments of the unwashed masses, this does not work.)

Here is the situation. Both players are acquainted with a reasonable knowledge of each other's skills. The effort begins at the negotiation of stakes and game format. During this bargaining, your opponent buys the first round of drinks.

About five to ten minutes before you would order a reciprocal round, he buys a fresh round of drinks. His response to this violation of behavior is a smile and a little lift of his glass that you enjoy. You are now two down.

In a break between games, your offer to order a round is declined. Some excuse is provided, "No, no. Two is my limit for the night." or "My wife always knows when I've had one too many." Your attempt is politely rebuffed. What was a minor social obligation now takes on greater importance in your mind.

During the end-game (the last couple of games in the match), one more drink magically appears. The score is now three and zero, with no way to "balance the books".

By the unwritten social rules, you are seriously in arrears. Your mind is now divided between concentrating on winning the match (with its prize) and the imbalanced obligations. Of additional concern is the chance you get tagged as a "taker" with no concern for proper social behavior.

Response

As a general personal standard of playing any competition - avoid consuming more than the single drink required in polite company. You must maintain a high level of alertness during the match. It doesn't do to lose because you had just a little too much alcohol.

In any match in this type of environment where even a small stake is at risk, the standards of behavior are usually well defined. Each person comes to the table with all of the attention focused on competing to the best of their abilities. Just because you are a nice guy, and wouldn't dream of attempting psychological tricks does not mean that your opponent follows your standards of chivalrous and knightly sportsmanship. Keep in mind that many of these social predators pay only lip service to social conventions.

As soon as the first drink arrives from your opponent, have one or more excuses ready at hand. For example, "My doctor only allows me one drink per day. Thank you." Or, "I get physically ill if I have more than one drink a day. Thanks anyway." This forces him to drink up both.

Here is a sneaky trick. Take a break between games, and on the way, order a drink (or even two) sent to your opponent. This kicks the whole social standard on its side.

Another way to prevent him from getting another round in is to leave the last drink untouched. (It is bad manners to buy a round when a full one is still in front of the recipient.) At the worst, you are only one down, which you can address after the match.

Emotional Opposites

Everyone has a routine emotional state that they live with day by day. Personal events may modify these stable living conditions – such as winning something, losing something, etc.

Some people walk around in a happy state of mine. They have a positive view on life in general, both at work and play. Other people walk around with a suppressed pissed-offness mindset. These are usually very impatient individuals, basically walking around looking for something to get upset or angry about. There are some who use the victimized attitude. Everything that goes wrong or makes their life tough is caused by something else outside of them or someone else's fault. These people couldn't take responsibility for getting to work on time.

The pool hustler who uses this shark can quickly identify your emotional state. Once he knows your general attitude, he can apply an opposite emotion. Most people are able to play decently as long as they are in their own mindset. When they compete against someone who is broadly applying an opposite personal attitude, it throws them off their game.

The hustler doesn't need to "feel" the emotional state he is demonstrating – he only needs to act it out. This outward appearance doesn't affect his playing skills. It is presented for the sole purpose of messing with your mind.

He can quickly pick up on your mental condition by watching your facial expressions and tone of voice. These provide sufficient clues to make a determination of which attitude he needs to apply against you.

Here are some examples and how he responds:

- You are happy with your life and work, bring to the table a positive approach. He assumes a sad and desolate personality, describing a tale of woe and worry about his recent trials and tribulations.

- You are on the downside – suspicious of others who might or could take advantage of you. He is all upbeat and enthusiastic. As such, he attempts to cheer you up and won't stop trying no matter what.

- You are quiet and contemplative, wanting to consider all things before making decisions, especially how to play the table layout. He is noisy and chatty, constantly talking and loudly disturbing the general atmosphere.

- You are exuberant and outgoing, willing to consider all people to be friendly (at least until proven otherwise). He is telling you to tone it down while complaining that he has a headache and is not interested in listening to your prattle about life.

- You are feeling upset and irritated, because something didn't go right. He is smiling and joking, oftentimes at your expense – all in a friendly sort of way – of course.

- You are full of optimism about life in general. He is expressing predictions of gloom and doom – designed to suppress your positive viewpoint.

Response

If you prefer a passive response to his efforts, stop communicating in any way. Assume your best poker-playing attitude. Nothing makes you happy. Nothing makes you sad. You play with no positive or negative emotions.

This stolid and emotionless game face affects his ability to carry on any peripheral conversations. Because the communication lines are cut off with your non-responsive attitude, his efforts begin to look a bit silly.

You can also try the meditative style. When it's not your turn, sit in your chair with eyes closed and assume a statue-like appearance. Let him remind you of your turn.

Try a variation of the "superior-above-it-all" approach. With a proper tone of voice, say, "How childish." A well-time sneer can be very effective in making him hate you.

"The Look" is also effective. On every conversational attempt - stop, stand up and direct an unblinking stare at your opponent. When you have eye contact, shake your head slowly for five seconds, followed by a return of your attention to the game.

Equipment Envy

This hustling trick is designed to affect the playing abilities of players who are envious of other people's possessions. It's a refinement that uses "Keep up with the Jones" psychological profiling. To make this work, the pool hustler MUST invest a significant amount of money into his pool tools.

Here is a real-life example of how one hustler basically over-awed his opponent. He laid out his beautiful custom designed and colored leather 3x5 case onto the table. Waiting a few minutes, he gauged the reactions of his opponent and the railbirds. The other player was immediately attracted to the case. He stepped up to the table and stared. The hustler started into his spiel.

He showed the genuine silver buttons, covered in gold chasing, originally from an old fancy Mexican saddle. He explained how the case was assembled from exotic leathers - alligator, ostrich, buffalo, etc., and how the pieces were colored. He encouraged his opponent and even the railbirds to feel the carvings – an offer eagerly accepted.

The hustler carefully went over every design feature and function – all of his personal design (natch). The many zippers, snaps, pockets, etc. were all opened for everyone's inspection.

Then, he pulled out the cue butts. One had fancy gold and silver filigree, another but was covered with a dragon made with mother of pearl. Each butt was a wonder of exotic woods, ebony, zebrawood, purple wood, etc. One of the cue butts has a ring of tiger eye stones embedded at the end. Even the shafts had a design swash inlaid just above the joint.

This guy was truly in love with his artwork – so it wasn't difficult for him to pull in his audience's attention. He knew that if he could dazzle his opponent enough, that he wouldn't have to work that hard to win games. And that was pretty much what happened. His opponent couldn't keep his eyes off the sticks and never really got down to seriously playing. He dropped a big bundle that day – and didn't really seem to mind the loss.

You might think that with such an ostentatious display, this guy was trying to cover up weaknesses in playing skills. He wasn't lacking in skill. However, he also didn't show off his best speed. He made very sure he didn't make spectacular shots – and often missed. But when the balls stopped rolling – his opponent usually had a rough table layout. Basically, his opponent got smoothly skinned.

Response

There aren't a lot of pool hustlers that have such an extensive and expensive set of fancy shooting equipment. But there are a few who have spent quite a bit of money. It is important not to be dazzled by the possessions of other players. However, when you do come up against someone who wants to engender jealousy and envy, you can easily turn this around and use the guy's pool stuff to shark him back.

Begin your response to his prideful presentation by being suitably impressed. Do this with continuous compliments on the work. Tell him how cool you think each of his possessions is. Follow this up with admiring statements over his design skills. Ask him how he came up with them and what they mean. (There's always a story.) There is no way you can over-exaggerate this ploy. He loves his gear way too much to realize that you are pulling him around by the nose.

The trick is to keep him continuously talking, thereby distracting his attention from the table. In addition, by stroking his ego, he gets too full of himself, which also decreases his abilities to concentrate on playing.

If, in the rare circumstance that this guy is able to pull his game together, there is another trick you can use. Ask to look at his cue stick again. Focus in on the very small details and closely inspect the artwork. Cue stick artists can be very sophisticated in general, but when getting down to details of the thickness of a hair, there are little discrepancies - maybe a slight roughness around an inlay, or an uneven application of lacquer, or a filigree curve that isn't smooth. As you point this out, say, "This is great work in general, but the details are somewhat flawed." Use similar statements. And yes, this is a mean trick. But stuck-up people need to have their ears pinned back once in a while.

Excessive Celebration

Some pool players seem to have never learned that celebratory behavior around a pool table should be understated or otherwise subdued. These individuals demonstrate excessive enthusiastic happiness for any success – minor or major. For those individuals, this can be their natural enthusiasm and reaction to success – maybe because of a lack of happy events away from the table. In all pool halls, there always seems to be one or two groups of players who get loud and noisy at various times.

For most players, the idea of "dancing in the end-zone" jubilations over a good play or win is worthy of being ostracized. Even the occasional loud and rousing cheer pushes the edges of tolerance for most shooters and even railbirds. A joyous up-thrust of the arm or a self-contained "whoop, whoop" is normally considered barely acceptable in the social norms around pool tables.

The more boisterous expressions of happiness and joy are often seen as unsportsmanlike behavior. After all, social standards need to be maintained, regardless of any internal joyful justification that is experienced. For the sake of good sportsmanship, the public face of most players is subdued and controlled.

There are times when you face a pool hustler who uses this inconsideration of social conventions as a tool of distraction. Such a person intentionally stretches the boundaries of tolerance. He doesn't have to be constantly celebratory. He only needs to perform his joyful exuberance enough to be unpredictable.

His occasions of expressed happiness are sudden and loud – enough to be startling to nearby individuals. He needs you to waste some of your game focus on watching him so as to not be shocked by an explosive joyful demonstration. The net result is that his very presence distracts your abilities to concentrate on game analysis and shooting processes.

Some of his tactical activities include:

• Dancing and spinning in place.

- Jumping up and down.

- Rapidly walking around the table getting high fives from anyone in his way.

- Loudly shouting "Whoo, whoo, whoo" while doing any of the above.

- Adding in the over-enthusiastic "Yippee" and "Yahoo" while doing a two-step jig.

The more exuberant he can be, the more it irritates you. To all observers, he cannot be publicly shamed in any way that could bring his actions under self-control. The pool hustler, of course, knows such actions and activities are out of place. That is his intention.

Response

You could try tripping him as he prances by, but that is really not recommended, since injury (possibly yours) could result. However, you can suddenly get in his way - the earlier in the dance the better. (If successful, you might even get a cheer from spectators.)

Don't use the same tactics as revenge. Any such behavior requires extensive practice and repetition. Another caution against duplicating his behavior is that so many people have cell phones to record any action considered interesting. You don't want to wake up the next day to discover you are the latest sensation on the social networks.

Instead, be stoic and calm. At opportunity, denigrate his childish behavior. If you can pull off a good sneer, throw that at him. Solicit negative commentary from railbirds. Publicly (in a loud voice) ask his friends how long has their buddy been this stupid or insane (extra points for getting a laugh from the railbirds).

Sometimes public ridicule can force an individual to dampen down behavior. If this is a league match, check with the team captains and see if they can somehow remonstrate with the guy. In a tournament, ask the TD (tournament director) to kick this guy out. If playing a pick-up game – simply case your stick and leave. Decent players should ostracize individuals with this type of playing personality.

Faking Poor Fundamentals

There are players, who when they first picked up a cue stick, developed bad habits and poor fundamentals. Some of them have become so enthusiastic about pool, they they've learned to shoot and play well anyway. But most players, when observed with poor fundamentals, are categorized as beginners and bar bangers. A pool hustler can often use this as a tool to win.

Grooving in the necessary muscle skills to automate this tactic requires a significant amount in practice time. It's like practicing an acting role. Few players would normally be interested enough to invest the time. But the master gamesman uses these so routinely, that any observer, however keen, would not realize it is a façade.

The presentation of this trick has to violate one or more of the basic shooting fundamentals. It can be bad feet positions, seemingly awkward grips on the stick, or some body movement during practice strokes. When well performed, watching these violations of best practices can mesmerize your attention.

Here are some examples, as observed by the author:

- While doing practice strokes, the upper body rises slightly with the forward movement of the cue stick. It looks like he is bobbing slightly on each back and forth. On the execution of the stroke, the body rises, and also leans into the shot. What you don't notice, is that this is done after the cue tip hits the cue ball.

- Gets down on the shot, lines up on a shot, and does a couple practice strokes. Then picks up his whole bridge hand and places it to the side for a couple more practice strokes. The bridge hand is moved back into position. Can be repeated several times before the actual shot is stroked. He's already got the shot lined up in his head. All of this is for show only.

- When doing practice strokes, pumps his elbow up and down. On the backstroke, the cue butt lifts up. On the forward stroke, the elbow drops. During the actual stroke, he is as solid as a tree.

- Shifts his weight alternately from the front foot to the rear foot and back, as he does his practice strokes. This rocking back and forth repeats until he executes the shot. You may not notice that just as he gets ready to stroke the shot, his weight is on his back foot.

- Sets up normally for a shot, but shifts his head side to side. Tilts his head one way and takes several practice strokes. Angles his head the other way and repeats. Eventually settles on something and shoots. He may also squint with one eye, like aiming a rifle.

- Sets up with an awkward stance, does some practice shots, and then rises up and come back down on the shot in a slightly modified position. Repeats this until he "gets it right".

When observing any of these gyrations, you may experience a slight tightening of stomach muscles in anticipation of his stroke execution. When he doesn't, and backs off on the shot, there's a slight feeling of disappointment.

To be fair, some players do have weird setups caused by ingrained bad habits enforced with years of playing. Somehow the problems were overcome enough for the shooter to become a good player. Regardless, whether any of these are intentionally designed to distract your attention or is an automatic routine, it is still disconcerting to watch.

Response

The solution is simple. Don't look at the execution of the shot. Focus your attention anywhere but on the playing area. Close your eyes, waiting to hear the click of the balls. Or perform some of those long-delayed maintenance tasks. Or, simply focus your attention on the action on another table. If you can't see any of these violations in fundamentals, you can't be bothered by them.

"Friendly" Insults

There are some hustlers who specialize in seemingly friendly insults – usually observed between two good friends. A player using this does not disguise his efforts with any subtleties.

He comes out with straight-forward statements of disrespect. He won't use the direct, in-your-face, intent-to-wish-you-harm insults, or the deadly defamations guaranteed to require friends on both sides to physically restrain the two of you. These are on the level of rude comments, with the occasional dig at your pride and jab in the bloomers.

These tributes to your lack of skills occur on every shot you have at the table. Even if you were successful, he finds some comment of un-appreciation. Each commentary is intended to test your reactions.

When he identifies a knee-jerk reaction from you, he flags as a useful tool to be used throughout the rest of the match and perhaps even in future competitions.

On the results of shots, he offers comments similar to this:

- What were you thinking about?
- I've never seen anything so far off target.
- Don't you put in any practice time?
- You must have had a brain-fart.
- You are shooting far below your skill level.
- Let me know when you get your game back.
- I am disappointed in you. I really thought you were a decent player.

Any of dozens of other comments, all on a similar theme, keep you from concentrating on playing your best. He can get personal too, insulting your hair style, clothes, and equipment.

Examples are "Who cut your hair? I want to stay away from that place." "I think I saw that shirt in a discount store for about $4.99. What did you pay?"

Silent insults are also available. On making a great shot, he says nothing and acts if it never happened. On a screw up, he catches your eye, shakes his head sadly, and does a slow, thumbs down.

He knocks your skills, rides your dignity, and vilifies your reputation. His creativity is only limited by his imagination. He probably spends hours searching the internet for insult dictionaries and put-down collections.

Response

You could provide the coldest shoulder possible, and proceed at your best pace. On a hustler using this shark, the effort would be wasted. Instead, try the blunt force approach to request. Loudly and directly ask that he be ever so quiet in the name of good sportsmanship. It's debatable whether this would work.

If you are clever and experienced at slinging insults, play the comeback insult game (common in schoolyard disagreements). Keep up the back and forth.

This distracts both of you from the game, but it can be fun. And, because you are initiating this distraction, you should recover faster and make some quick gains while he is still reeling from your volleys.

If you happen to be around when two players are involved in an insult/counter-insult challenge, stick around and soak up some of the exchanges. You might pick up several good ones to be remembered for the next time you need a few zingers.

Gayness

This is a shark that requires practice to ensure its presentation is smooth and easy to implement without any rough edges. It needs some sort of video recording device (video camera or a smart phone) to ensure that this trick is performed well.

The key to making this shark work requires that the hustler's opponent have some kind of unconscious reaction to "gay" behavior. Intellectually and socially, most people have the Politically Correct attitude about that life style.

But for some people, putting the behavior right in front of their nose could trigger an unconscious reaction – usually more of an increase in space between the two individuals.

When a pool hustler seems an opponent who has this unconscious response to gay behavior, this trick can be used to intentionally distract the concentration and focus – making a match win that much easier to accomplish.

There are several ways a pool hustler can use this shark. It's isn't necessary to be a full-blown fairy. All that is needed is to create the impression. One tactic is the wearing of a brightly colored and patterned shooting glove.

Generally, this glove design is used by women, who often like light, bright colors – plain or with a pattern. Guys, being guys, usually wear black or dark brown shooting gloves.

When the hustler identifies that as a possibly effective trick, on putting on the glove, he checks to see if you look at it. If you show any kind of interest, however mild, he begins telling you a story about a seamstress friend of his.

He'll say, she makes them up from interesting stretchy colorful material. And because he likes the way it looks when he puts his bridge hand onto the table cloth, he explains this as the reason why he carries several with him. He'll even pull out three or four to show.

If the glove is commercially made, he explains that it was the prettiest that he could find. You may even get a story about how he searched and searched and finally found it on a web site in Europe. The intention is for you to glue your eyes to his glove every time he gets down on a shot. This, of course, keeps your mind distracted for the table layout and prevents effective analysis.

Another aspect of this shark is done during the introductions and the obligatory hand shaking with good lucks all around. He does not present the firm grip recommended by John Wayne and Clint Eastwood.

Instead, you are on the receiving end of a slightly limp-wristed hand with a weak grasp. A welcoming smile is included, along with something like, "It is sooo <extended length intended> nice to meet you." If you still weren't sure if he was putting some moves on, right as he grips your hand, he pulls it towards you slightly and quietly says, "I hope you enjoy the game." Only then does is his grip released.

His game play proceeds as if nothing happened. If you start getting your game on, he can add other distractions. For example, as he walks by your chair during his turn, he might hesitate and throw you a wink.

If you have any kind of observable reaction, these jabs continue throughout the match. He pays very close attention to your reactions throughout the match. One trick or another is used to keep you concerned.

Response

If you are somewhat bothered by these intentional come-ons, you are playing into his hands. Shrug it off. If the guy is what he is indicating, nothing you can do is going to change anything in his attitude or behavior. Focus all of your attention on the table, ignoring any conversational attempt he may try.

You can also do the ignoring tactic. While he is shooting, close your eyes and pretend to doze off in your chair. Force him to remind you to play. You can also watch a game at another table or get into a deep conversation with any railbird.

This is a one act play. If the shark doesn't appear to be working, it is quickly dropped. The pool hustler is thrown off his game slightly on realizing this trick's failure, so you should have time to concentrate on the game and advance closer to the win.

Generation Gap

This tactic is commonly used by older players (qualified AARP members) on younger shooters (20-somethings). They are fulfilling an obligation to the past and the future. When they were young, they were victims of the oldsters. Now that they have joined the gray hair league, it is their obligation to use those same tricks on today's youth. Basically, what they suffered decades ago, they pass onto the next generation.

Any young person likes to believe that he is mature enough to handle his own affairs without interference from "old folks". Add in the desperate need to look cool (or at least not a dork) to his peers and that individual is a walking bulls-eye.

Here is an example of how this shark is applied. A kid is looking around for someone to play. An old geezer notices his search for an opponent and volunteers. The shark begins before the match.

The older guy starts with a fixed stare at the younger player. The kid finally responds with "What?" With a wondering and curious tone of voice, old dude asks, "Did you really pay money for that *<haircut, shirt, etc.>*?" There is a slight pause, then the zinger, "It doesn't look good on you. Who are you trying to impress?"

Further into the match, additional input is offered, "What did you spend on those clothes? Can you get your money back?" He then patiently waits for the reactions, hiding his little smile as the response takes effect.

A few minutes later, he switches over to the hair-do and says, "I suppose that haircut can grow out in a month or two. You probably should wear a hat for a while."

These and other comments and questions dig deep into the kid's psyche. The old guy knows, since he was the same target long ago. Each verbal thrust is closely monitored for effectiveness. Positive results are noted when observing a slight tightening of the lips, a passing frown or a roll of the eyes. Additional prods help keep the youngster off balance.

If there is someone of a similar age at a nearby table, the oldster tells the kid (quietly of course) just how stupid that youngster looks. Additional comments speculate about probable upbringing, such as, "Looks like his parents have some kind of degenerative brain disease to let him look like that." Even though targeted at someone else, the kid still feels the effects as a back-handed insult.

For the old-timer, this is pure personal entertainment and an opportunity for revenge against the flow of time. It is his way of passing on the suffering that his old dudes gleefully used to put down him and his buddies. Now he is gifted with this opportunity to be just as witty as they were back then.

NOTE: This is strictly a one-way street for the youngster. To take his revenge, he has to let a few decades go by before he can inflict the same sharks on that new generation.

Response

If you happen to spot such a competition between generations, stop to enjoy the show. It can be entertaining to watch the expertise in which the oldster disintegrates the focus and concentration of his target.

Young players all need some seasoning and it is a social obligation for senior citizens to provide this type of education. It might even be considered a right and privilege of getting old.

If this is happening to you as the younger player, grow up and use your head. You are not your clothes or haircut. In any competition on the pool table, you are a player.

Smile to the elderly gentleman and thank him for the opinion. Then focus your attention on the game. Use the pokes that attempt to distract you to drive your focus and intention to be the winner.

Health Queries

This shark is designed to seriously consider whether your health is may not be as good as you thought – and maybe you need to have a serious discussion with your medical practitioner. This trick is a diversionary tactic to redirect some of your game focus from the competition onto thoughts and worries about your personal abilities to be alive tomorrow. If you are an introspective personality, this can be very effective. If you are a hypochondriac, it would be easier to pay up and go home.

It starts when the pool hustler extends his hand for the regular greeting of competitors before the match begins. As the introductions are completed and the appropriate wishes for a competitive match (i.e., "Let's have fun kicking each other's butts." or some other pleasantry), he holds his grip on your hand for a fraction of a second longer, staring intently into your face. At the moment of release, he says something like, "You look in good shape but ..." and leaves the sentence dangling in mid-air. He pauses for a couple seconds, nods to himself, and then turns away.

The conversation proceeds with:

<you> "What?"

<he> "Did you just recover from an illness?"

<you> "No. Why?"

<he> Somewhat vaguely, "You look a little off. I'm not sure. *<pause>* Could be nothing. *<pause>* Are you sure you weren't sick the last couple of months?"

<you> "I'm sure. Nothing wrong with me."

<he> "Fine - fine. Don't worry about it. Let's play."

Forced by curiosity, you might press the point. He responds with, "Well, it looks like you are a bit tired. You seem to be, maybe a bit pale, too."

And this is when you fall into his trap. By asking questions about his rationale for these statements, you have just given him the match.

With your encouragement, he may offer suggestions for rest and relaxation, trips to spas, etc. If you are particularly insistent on clarification, he has you thinking about how soon you can get to your doctor or even wonder if it might be better to go straight to the emergency room.

The pool hustler needs to appear to be somewhat knowledgeable. This only needs an apparent understanding of medical vocabulary. This is easy to do with a couple hours of casual reading on the WebMD site. The preparation is all that is needed to add gravitas to his medical ramblings. He may even say he has experience as a health care advisor.

Nodding sagely, he opines, "I have seen something like this before. One person I talked with followed my advice to get a checkup and discovered some problems with his red cell count. If he hadn't checked, he might have died." Here he is implying that the checkup was based on his suggestions, but never actually states it was someone's routine test.

Response

Whenever you let a pool hustler guide your thinking patterns, you become susceptible to his influences. This shark is intended to guide your thinking – but only if you let it.

As soon as you recognize that this is another distraction trick, it is easy to guide his conversation away from yourself and onto someone else. Start doing some digging. "You are an experienced expert. Do you know about <something>." Start asking for medical opinions about a friend's sleeping problems or a relative's digestive disagreements.

His efforts to internalize your focus appear pretty weak once you are on the offensive. You can actually continue this process and put him entirely on the defensive – to the point where he desperately looks for an escape.

One advantage of this medical aggression is that he goes on the defensive, throwing off his ability to play well. Anytime it looks like his game is coming together, ask another health question.

Helpfulness

It's nice to have good allies and advisors around you. These people can help improve your life and life style. But on the pool table, do NOT expect your opponent to be one of the individuals who have your best interests at heart. There are two reasons why an opponent would provide help and guidance. One, you are not a threat to his pocket book or self-esteem, or two, he wants to enfeeble your intentions to win.

During the match, the pool hustler assumes a very helpful attitude. He has nothing but good wishes for your success, and happily assumes the role of your pool playing mentor and professional instructor.

Every time you are at the table, he turns that into a teaching moment. He becomes your guide to better shot choices, better shooting fundamentals, better everything. Whatever the table situation, he is there with an idea or suggestion – to help, of course.

For example, you have an easy shot on a jawed ball. He explains the correct applied cue ball spin and speed to get the cue ball into position for the next shot. And, of course, if you haven't practiced and mastered cue ball side spin or speed control, the result is not as intended.

If you have a more difficult shot, he provides tips on bisecting angles, calculating the aiming line, plus several possible ways to play the shot. He even helps line up the shot.

You get a lot of guidance on offensive efforts. And all his recommendations and suggestions are truthful. It's not his fault you lack the experience to do the shot as his explains.

You won't get any guidance on when, why, and how you should play a defensive shot. The silence is deafening. And if you ask for help, his answers provide limited and minimal details. Defensive ideas and concepts is not something he wants you to learn.

The problem is this: when you start listening to your opponent, you stop thinking for yourself. You quickly become dependent on his thinking to decide what shot to shoot and how to play the table. When that happens, you also stop analyzing whether his ideas are good for you. There are two dangers:

- He can very subtly shade his advice so that you are not shooting the best choice. Any unsuccessful effort is easily blamed on your poor execution, while he says, "Well, I tried my best."

- He can stop providing help. Even with a small dependency on his support, the sudden cut-off requires some time to get your brain out of neutral. During that time, he can easily win several games.

Response

Think about the idea of your opponent helping you beat him. Why would he ever be serious about doing that? Of what benefit would he gain from assisting you to win?

Do you really want advice from someone who has money on the table (of any amount)? You are better off persuading him to stop bothering you with his advice. Once you can start playing without his kindly considerations, you can get back to properly doing your own thinking and learning from successes and failures.

Only when you handle your own problems do you gain the value of the experience and lessons learned from the consequences. If a playing decision works well, you have some practical experience on what works for that situation. If it goes wrong, you can add little guidelines, such as, "Don't do that again." or "Put a little more (or less) speed on that type of shot." Making your own choices is also necessary to mature in your shooting and playing skills, mental and physical.

If the hustler is persistent about providing his knowledge, say, "I appreciate your help. How about we set up a time when you can give me some lessons and instruction?" If he really is competent, that is when you want to pick his brains.

If you do need advice, suggestions, or ideas; ask known allies. You can trust their motivations and intentions.

How & Why

This shark is designed to interrupt the continuity of your game focus. The pool hustler begins this scheme by establishing an apparent over-anxious desire to improve himself. He exhibits some minor flaws in his fundamentals, such as gripping the cue butt a little too far back, getting down in a slightly awkward stance, setting up a shot with a bridge that is too long, or any of a dozen minor problems.

He starts by offering a series of compliments to you, along the lines of, "I've checked around and you are one of the well-respected players." and "I've admired your stroke for quite some time. It sure is smooth." He leads with several simple questions that can be answered easily with a yes or no and without extended explanations.

- How tight should I grip my stick?

- Are my feet in the correct positions?

- Is my stance OK?

- Is this a good bridge?

The next stage is a series of questions that do require some extra thinking and more detailed answers. These types of questions now relate to your skills.

- How did you draw like that?

- How do you know how hard to hit the cue ball?

- What kind of English was that?

- How did you make that shot?

The next stage involves hitting you with "Why" questions. These are usually activities that you have automated and give little thought or consideration.

- Why did you hit that so hard?

- Why did you hit that so soft?

- Why did you use that English?

By this point, your game concentration is minimal and you are lucky if you can plan to make, much less actually pocket two balls in a row.

The final level of distractive questions is rarely needed. The earlier levels are usually more than sufficient to cause you to plan and play poorly. He begins asking why you selected certain shots, but only after the results were obviously disastrous. This keeps your attention on failures.

There are several results that the pool hustler wants to create during the match.

- First, as you listen to his questions, your attention is on him and not the table. This makes it difficult to perform a proper table analysis.

- Second, he wastes game time, which throws off your playing rhythms.

- Third, with your game focus thrown off kilter, it is more difficult to concentrate on properly playing each shot.

Your ongoing strategic thinking is being continuously interrupted. You are forced to only consider the immediate tactical problems based on the table layout. Without a strategic plan to tie together your tactical decisions, your chances of winning are reduced.

Response

Do not get sucked into actually giving advice, no matter how nice and innocent and friendly your opponent tries to present himself. No matter how flattering his compliments and respect are to your ego, why would you help your opponent win money from you?

If you want to keep it friendly, ask him how much time he thinks it takes to learn *<whatever question he asked>*. Then say it took you about ten or twenty times that long. Alternately, when he presents a question, give a short answer. Then request that he pay a fee ($5, $10, or $20).

In a serious competition, be blunt. A little rude is OK, such as, "Figure it out yourself." Also try, "Not my problem."

Ignoring

This is a subtle gambit that attempts to ostracize or somehow exclude you from general membership in the human race. It is rarely seen in local and regional tournaments and competitions, but can be observed in professional matches.

This begins at the introductions. During the introduction, the hustler does not acknowledgement your existence. His eyes avoid contact with you. Even his body position is slightly turned away. If he does shake your hand, it is done mechanically and with no hand pressure. Below are several ways that he won't pay attention to you.

While seated:

- With eyes closed, totally ignoring your presence.

- With eyes open, completely ignores the table activity while you are shooting.

- Requires you to constantly inform him of his turn at the table.

Other ostracizing efforts include:

- Conversations with someone else, usually with his back to the table.

- Watches other tables with mild interest.

- Reading a book.

- Walking away from the table.

- Ignoring all of your conversational attempts.

Every time you complete your turn, you are forced to get his attention to begin his turn. Sometimes you have to raise your voice, other times you might have to walk directly in front of him. With no acknowledgement of your attempt to keep the game going, he simply picks up his stick and goes to the table.

He never looks in your direction or says anything to you. There is no eye contact, facial expression, or any other indication that you are a living, breathing human being.

This shark is distracting in two ways. One is the total disregard for your existence. The other is the extra work you have to do to constantly remind him of his turn.

Response

The passive response would be to just live with the problem and get through the match as best you can. Accept the fact that you have to do something each time you finish your turn.

There are proactive options. One is to use physical interactions instead of verbal notifications. Extend your cue stick out in front of him and wave it around. If this elicits no reaction, allow the cue to tap his knee, just enough to be noticeable. Extra point if he appears irritated by this method.

Test to see how far he wants to take this trick. Instead of reminding him, when your turn is over, quietly retire to your chair and wait. If he gets up within a few seconds, he was paying attention. Make sure to laugh about it. If he stays apparently ignorant – take your own nap.

Make it a comparison of wills, wait him out. One choice is this: if nothing happens after about five minutes, pack up and leave. If any money was on the table, pick it up as you leave. Another choice is to grab up the cue ball and claim it as a ball-in-hand penalty for delaying the game.

There is another very effective response to this shark. When you miss, stand near the table with a thoughtful attitude. After about 45 seconds, continue shooting. If he is way too inattentive, you can continue until you win the game. If he immediately jumps up to claim the foul – laugh at him. This should resolve the game onto a normal competitive tone.

Injuries

To apply this duplicity, the hustler either suffers or fakes the suffering of some physical limitation that restricts body movement. The goal is to get you to take him less seriously as a competitor. If you fall for this trick, you even slack off on your usual game intensity.

The assumption on observing an injured competitor is that he won't be able to compete well. Therefore, by default, you fall into the trap of thinking that your opponent is less than normally capable.

This assumption is based on your lifetime experiences in other competitive sports – basketball, football, baseball, rugby, soccer, etc. Playing "hurt" in billiards is not the same as with more physical sports. Your automatic consideration has less real-world reality.

The attempt to lull your competitive spirit begins when the two of you shake hands at the start of the match. Your opponent approaches you with slow and obvious physical restrictions. He may even wince during the hand clasp.

Each movement is an example of slow and careful planning of how different body parts are moved and shifted.

Your adversary won't volunteer any details about why he is so obviously hampered. He intends to give the impression of a brave and gallant competitor regardless of any personal limitations (for the love of the game, of course).

When you can no longer hold back your curiosity, and finally ask about it, he grudgingly provides a short minimal explanation. To get more details, you need to continuously badger him.

The story that emerges involves some seemingly miraculous escape from a potentially deadly circumstance, resulting in only this minor souvenir. Or, it can be an injury suffered while performing a heroic act such as saving a kitty or puppy.

On finishing an explanation of his self-inflicted heroism, he implies that you should take it a little easy on him since he is struggling with his handicap.

The story, plus the careful adjustments to play (so as to not aggravate the injury) appear to validate the claim. Even a partial buy-in to the effort takes some of the edge off your game. This must be well presented and requires some practice in front of a mirror to provide just the right level of suffering.

Even if the injury was real, it can be further exaggerated for effect. A sore toe (stubbed on a night-time trip to the refrigerator?) results in intensive hobbling.

Appropriate medical accessories, etc. can be included to add some veracity. When presented by an expert, the acting is of Oscar quality. He can get you to feel so sorry for him that you apologize for getting temporarily ahead in the match.

Response

Do not be sympathetic. In fact, the more unsympathetic you can be, the more you can get him upset over your seeming callousness. Even if he is faking, you should be able to get him irritated over your lack of concern.

If you don't mind a little "in your face" work, tease him on his foolishness on getting injured. You can also tell him you are happy to accept a default win from him.

Check for fakery. Closely watch his routines and execution. Look for lapses in his act, such as effortlessly moving around or leaping from his chair to take an easy advantage you accidentally gave up.

If you can't catch him in an obvious forgetful moment, become over-solicitous. Constantly ask if he needs help. Go over and offer a hand to assist him out of a chair. Constantly be attentive and concerned about his health.

Even if he does have some kind of real injury that he's enhancing, his constant response to your solicitations go far to throw him off his game.

Invisible Friend

When this psychological tactic is well-played, your first thought is to wonder if your opponent really might be insane. On second thought, you might consider whether he might live a more fulfilling life under 24/7 supervision. Finally, you realize that if this was a serious problem, someone else would have handled the situation long before today.

In this hustle, your opponent is shadowed by his invisible friend with whom he has continuous discussions about the game. He carries on analysis discussions with his companion as he develops various strategies and tactics. His conversation goes something like this:

"Well, George *<name picked at random>*. What do you think?" *<pause for an invisible answer>*

"I like that. If I start with the 3 ball with some top left I should be able to line up on the 4. And a short draw should get me to the 7 ball. Pretty good idea." *<pause for an invisible comment>*

"That's right. Half speed should do it. I don't want to hit the ball too hard." *<pause for another invisible comment>*

"I'm glad you agree." *<pause>*

"What?" *<pause>* "Yeah, I keep forgetting to do that. Thanks."

And he gets down, runs through a regular set-up routine, and fires off the shot.

The trick can be further enhanced by a clever hustler. It is extended into heated arguments about tactics and shooting choices. He may even have a tiff resulting in a length of silence. Periodically, he says," I'm ignoring you. Go away." If you ask about his "buddy", you get a response similar to, "I'm not talking to George. He's too damn stubborn for his own good." The tiff is fixed up as the match proceeds. Then the conversations continue.

He can even include you in this shark – as a topic of discussion. They talk about you as if you were the invisible person. The conversation proceeds along these lines, "Who am I playing?" *<pause>* "Oh, sorry. I didn't introduce you. That's *<your*

name>?." <pause> "What do you mean he doesn't know how to draw?" *<pause>* "Oh yeah, he did blow that shot."

Any questioning as to who his quiet friend is leads to a refusal to provide details. The success of this distraction depends on his ability to act in character. Even when poorly done, the play-acting keeps you from fully focusing on your game.

That's all he needs to do with this trick – keep you from focusing your total attention on winning. Remember, just because he acts crazy, doesn't mean his playing ability is also weak.

Response

If you want to pursue the passive reaction to this shark, simply enjoy the conversational exchanges. Ignore the behavior; just proceed at your best speed. His efforts can't distract you if you don't get pulled into his act.

If you find your attention moving away from the table and onto his activities, you need to be proactive. The most effective response is to participate in his dialog.

Wait for an entry into his conversation, and then try something like, "No, no. He's wrong! With that stroke you're going to end up over in the corner. Use a medium hard stroke at 4:30 and go back and forth to end up on the 4 ball." Make sure all of your conversation contributions are real suggestions. Just sticking in your two cents with any silly statement gets you glared at by both your opponent and his invisible friend. The idea with proactive participation is force his attention away from the table – a good counter-measure.

This also forces him to place more effort into maintaining and defending his distractive efforts. While he is burning up his limited attention span, you can advance towards the win.

Jokes

This tactic uses your own appreciation of humor to prevent you from playing with all due intelligence and intention. You have an adversary who is a wanna-be comedy club regular. He is accustomed to being the center of attention of any group that he joins. To him, the game is just another venue for his funny presentations. You are another of his many audiences - only one person, to be sure - but to his viewpoint, still a qualified (and captive) public spectator.

The amateur usually has problems timing the delivery of the punch lines for the maximum destruction of your focus. He doesn't take into account your game rhythm. As a result, he finishes too early or too late for the best reactions. The variety of his repertoire is equally limited. His routine is exhausted by the end of the first couple of games. Even so, a few of the jokes might be good enough to cause problems for your due diligence.

Over the years, the expert user of this shark has honed the style and delivery to achieve the maximum impact and distractive results. His collection of jokes is immense, garnered from years of being the class clown and the designated entertainer of his group of friends.

He has a variety of clean jokes suitable for any church social. He has a selection of suggestive jokes for mixed company. For guys-only situations, he knows enough dirty jokes to keep everyone in stitches for a couple of hours.

First, the hustler figures out your personal playing rhythm. That allows him to tailor the joke to have its greatest effect on you. Most commonly, he times the delivery of the gag line to arrive when you should be concentrating on table analysis and making tactical selections. Any resulting laughter destroys game focus and playing routines are disrupted.

The greater the success of the joke, the longer it takes you to get restarted. Without proper concentration on the game, you cannot maintain the serious intent needed to get to the win. That is what he wants to accomplish.

He doesn't have to be a stage comedian with joke after joke. He only needs to distract you at key points in the match. In some cases, all he needs is a single good joke to throw off any momentum.

Response

Don't try to out-joke him or get into any "who is funniest" efforts. He has far more experience being the center of attention and the designated clown. Instead, try making a big deal about having respect for the "Game".

Explain that the competition is a place to show the courtesy of good sportsmanship and respect between opponents. Include an appeal that he has some consideration for those playing on other tables.

If that doesn't work, stay in your chair when it is your turn and wait for him to begin his latest joke. Hustlers using the joking shark have a hard time enduring silence without an attempt to fill it.

The trick is to lean forward as if to get to your feet so that he starts the joke. Then lean back and let him finish. Because his jokes are timed to your regular playing rhythm, staying seated ensures your attention to the game is not affected.

Dutifully laugh at the delivery of the punch line. (This also throws off his timing and delivery because you are not acting normally.)

Only get up to play when you have regained control of your intention to win. Once that is in place, take over the table. If he tries to start another joke, hold up your hand in the stop signal, then place your index finger against your lips in the "shh" sign.

Basically, throw him off his timing. This makes him a bit uncertain about when and how to start his next joke. While he is in this minor state of confusion, you can advance your game. Changing and adjusting your routine screws up his rhythm.

Jump Starting

This little hustling trick is designed to confuse and destroy your playing rhythm. It is most affective on players who have a passive response to people – the "go along to get along" attitude. If you are such an individual who uses this to help survive life, this is very effective.

Here is how the hustler gets this started. He stays seated and silent (good sportsmanship on display). But the instant he determines that your turn is over, he literally leaps up to begin his turn. The balls are usually still moving when he springs into action. If you happen to be in his way to the table, he crowds past you as if this was some kind of emergency. He may say "excuse me", but only as an afterthought. The time he spends on table analysis, setup, and execution routines are also similarly accelerated.

Another tactic is for him to stand just off to the side of your shooting position. He won't move, assuming the picture of patience. Then, the instant you shoot, he suddenly moves, on the assumption that you missed. In your peripheral vision, this attracts your attention, taking your eyes off the table, even as the balls are moving. Even if you make the shot, your concentration is messed up.

While you are shooting, he can also display little signs of impatience (i.e., toe tapping, fidgeting, knuckle cracking, etc.) Even when you don't see his impatience, you know it's there – another bit of pressure on you to hurry up.

On your shot completion, as he suddenly jerks into movement, he is covered both ways. If you miss, he is hurriedly walking around the table, concentrating on the layout. If you make it, he (again hurriedly) moves to the other side of the table. Either way – you notice this and lose a certain amount of concentration. About half the time, he is at the edge of your peripheral vision.

When playing pool, there is no need to react instantly - for example, ping pong, tennis, football, and other games where quick responses are necessary to properly play the game. Pool has a certain quiet flow of the way players move around.

Therefore, anyone acting as if the game required quick reactions creates a significant change in the general playing atmosphere. By being put under this "reactive" pressure, you unconsciously tend to speed up yourself. You get off-balance and become slightly confused. And this state of mind is what the hustler wants. There is nothing illegal about it, even with the most stringent rules.

Response

You do not want to allow his "hurry-up" offense to force a change in your playing rhythm. If you begin speeding up normal routines, there is less time to consider all the table options. Your normal rhythm suits your thinking processes. Being forced to spend less time in consideration translates to poorer quality choices, causing mistakes and judgment errors.

Instead of acquiescing to his implied pressure to "speed it up", use the opposite approach - slow down even more. When it is your turn, take an extra 10-15 seconds to study the table before you move. Contemplate the table from the comfort of the sidelines or your chair - and do so for an extended period of time. If he tries to encourage you to rush, look at him with a calm and patient gaze (for several seconds). Just when he is ready to say something, speak up, "I'll be ready when I'm ready, *<pause 2 seconds>* and not before." You would be amazed how quickly he gets short tempered with this tactical response – which affects him game.

An alternative is to use false starts. For example, take a couple of quick steps from your chair, then stop and assume a pose of contemplation. After about 7-10 seconds, move to the other side of the table and repeat.

Here is another tactical response - when considering a tough table layout (about 10-12 seconds), turn to him and ask, "What would you do with this?" Regardless of his response (positive or negative), you have momentarily changed his thinking patterns. An extra point if you manage to force a considered opinion from him.

The standing stare also works. When you see him leaning forward in his chair for his sudden movement, stop your shot, stand up, and ask, "What?" Stare at him for a few seconds, then return to your standard playing routine.

Late to Begin

Have you ever gone out with someone who was constantly and consistently late in getting ready to go or meeting you someplace? Remember that sense of frustration as you waited impatiently with nothing to do but count seconds to keep busy? That is just a feeling your opponent wants you to experience with this distractive effort.

This is most often seen in tournament play. A variation of this can be used during casual or pick-up games. In all tournaments, the pace of the event depends on individual competitions getting started within a certain time frame; usually a set number of minutes after the names of the competitors and the playing table are called out. The general rule is: if one of the players does not show up within that period of time, the person who is at the table is awarded the win and the no-show player forfeits the match.

An unprincipled opponent waits in the background through the second and third call for the match players. He carefully tracks the time on his wristwatch. Then, just before the final seconds pass for the forfeit to be declared, the guy magically appears at the playing area, ready to go. He might fake a little huffing and puffing to make his delay seem more reasonable.

Upon being called to the table, you are already feeling a little nervous about the competition. You might be vigorously rubbing a good luck charm, or saying a little positive thinking mantra in your head, such as, "I'm gonna win, I'm gonna win, etc.".

During that waiting period for your opponent to show up, you go through several emotional experiences. At the beginning, you stride to the table, full of confidence and filled with purposeful intent. Your mind is focused on the competition. Toss in some nervous anticipation to the mix.

Halfway through the waiting period, the thought does occur that your opponent might not show up – maybe suffering a collision with a truck while entering the pool hall and already be on his way to the hospital. You relax slightly, because holding yourself in readiness is physically exhausting. When the final couple minutes starts ticking away, hope for a match forfeit and the easy win rises in your heart. The closer to the final seconds, the greater is your expectation and anticipation.

Just as you consider this to be your match, your opponent shows up - looking fit, exuding confidence, and ready to battle for the right to advance in the tournament.

A sudden hole opens up in the pit of your stomach. Your mind scrambles frantically to adjust from the positive pleasures of certain victory to the realization that you really must re-install your game attitude. That's a lot of shock to the system.

Having suffered this roller coaster ride of emotional expectations, it is not difficult to quickly lose the first few games before your get your focus and concentration back into place.

Response

You need time to recover time to change mental directions. To allow yourself the necessary time to get back into the competitive mood, slow down everything you do.

- Walk slowly and deliberately.

- Take extra time to analyze the table layout.

- Perform a longer than usual pre-shot routine.

- When you execute the shot, regardless of its results, stay in place to analyze the rights and wrongs of the attempt.

- Take your time, repeat. Take your time, repeat.

This is how you regain control of your inner game. An additional side benefit is that it also acts as a distractive effort to your opponent.

As you gain control over your game, you can also frustrate his intentions to get ahead quickly and easily. Look for signs of irritation (grimace, tightened lips, and/or frown). If you see any of these soon after you begin the reassembly of your focus, continue those activities long after you are back into the spirit of the game.

Lingering

This distractive shark is designed to test the far reaches of your patience during the time when your opponent finishes his turn and your turn begins. Depending on how smoothly he can present this delay, he can prevent the beginning of your turn from 30 seconds to two minutes. This trick is designed to create a timing obstacle. It prevents you from being able to immediately take control of the table after your opponent misses.

Here is how the hustler pulls this off. When he completes his shot, he does not immediately move away to leave the playing area available for you. Instead, he either freezes in place while down on the last shot – or arises from the shot and assumes the standing version of the same facial expression as Auguste Rodin's "The Thinker" statue. For a considerable length of time, he silently stares over the table and the consequences of his last shot.

While in this pose, a few minor movements (a slight turn of the head, weight shift to one foot, etc.) may occur to indicate he is still alive. Looking closely, you might see his lips moving silently, and perhaps the twitch of a finger as it traces out an imaginary pattern. Except for that he is buried in intense concentration and totally oblivious to the world.

He continues this until he appears to reach some kind of conclusion. Only then does he come back into himself and time begins to run normally - at least for him. For you, it has been an interminable period of impatient waiting. He may not even realize he's been holding up your turn. If he does, he moves off while extending his deep apologies. Otherwise, he casually saunters off to his waiting area. Either way, the damage is done.

If you try to interrupt him to encourage his exit, he puts you off with, "Just a minute. I'm trying to figure out something here." A repeated request from you is also rebuffed. It's not like you can march up to him and rudely shoulder him aside.

He won't perform this process at every turn. But it always occurs in the middle of an important part of the game. It is especially distracting if he has left you with an easy opportunity to advance. The more you want to get out there and make it happen, the more he imitates the patience of a statue. He also uses this when it looks like you are on a roll or are getting ahead. By interrupting the beginning of your turn, he is working to modify your rhythm.

True, some people do this same activity as they perform a mental review to figure out what went wrong, but it is usually complete within moments. As a distractive tactic, this careful game delay extends the time frame of his turn and delays your approach to the table. The trick is designed to prevent you from advancing onto the field of battle with mind filled with strategic/tactical considerations to a mindset of barely constrained impatience at his delay in leaving the table area.

The results are cumulative. The irritations of each lingering attempt pile onto each previous effort. As the match proceeds, your irritation grows to the point where he only has to stand still for a few seconds and he has trained you to begin a new habit of muttering obscenities.

Response

Once you identify this type of delaying tactic, there are a couple of different things you can do. One option is to apply the same tactic to him. Whatever he does to delay your turn, you duplicate to delay his turn. Of course, if he is stubbornly persistent, a single game could take 20-30 minutes. But if you have enough intestinal fortitude, you can out wait him to the point where he is so frustrated, the match is an easy win.

Alternately, stay in your seat and remain relaxed. When your opponent finally does return to his chair (however long that takes), remain there until he notices that you are not getting up and around. Require him to inform you of your turn.

If you want to be proactive, come up behind him while he is deep in thought. Tap his shoulder several times to get his attention. When he turns around, jerk your thumb towards his chair. If he hesitates, repeat the gesture.

Listening

You would think that a key requirement of any sharking trick is to intrude on your thoughts. But this apparently innocent tactic is a destroyer of focus if you are the type of person who likes to inform others about your opinions and viewpoints. A knowledgeable gamesman, well trained in applied psychology, immediately recognizes your personality type and uses this very effective tactic. All he has to do is appear to be a genial fellow whose only purpose in life is to find you and become your confidant. His intent and purpose is to get you talking, a lot.

There is a common saying, "To appear wise, disengage mouth, and engage brain." In other words, if you want to learn something - simply shut up and pay attention. The converse of this little morsel of enlightenment is simple, "To make bad decisions, spend too much time talking." Basically, the brain can't consider results and consequences when the mouth is being used.

The entirety of his effort is to significantly decrease your analysis skills. The hustler's question is: how can he convince you to not do a proper table analysis? Easy - make sure you are too busy talking about something - anything.

A hustler, coming into a pool hall, can quickly identify the personality styles of everyone in the pool hall with just a few moments of observation. Once he knows whether someone is outgoing, talkative, quiet, depressed, happy, etc., he has lined up a set of sharks, ready to apply to each individual.

Having identified you as too talkative, he begins with the usual introductions. His first comments are along the lines of, "Hello. My name is *<some name>*. I've heard good things about you." This and other seemingly minor compliments immediately get you started.

Essentially, you voluntarily step into his trap. You might ask, "So what have you heard?" He responds with some general compliments, such as, "You're a decent player and a good all-around competitor." With this confirmation and invitation, you first bask in a moment of self-congratulations, and then proceed to take over the conversation.

As needed, he provides leading questions to keep you going. These examples are pool-related, but he adapts them to whatever subject you are rambling on about.

- How old were you when you first started playing?
- What was it like?
- Who have you played with?
- What are some of the other places in the world you played?
- How often do you practice?
- What do you like best about this sport?

Because this intelligent individual obviously has an attentive set of ears, your appreciation and respect of your opponent rises. Any request for more details are happily provided.

Response

Everyone appreciates the occasional opportunity to brag up oneself to an obviously keen listener. If you are blinded by your own ego, you probably won't realize you were sharked until long after the match is over. And if you realize that you are spending too much time talking and not enough time thinking, he has a significant lead in games. It's like giving him a huge handicap.

As a general rule in any match, do NOT get friendly with an adversary before and during a match. It is very important that you constantly remember "there are no friends on the table".. If you can catch yourself spewing verbal diarrhea, take responsibility for your stupidity and put all of your attention get back into the competition. Stop all communications and only offer simple grunts, as needed.

This is a type of hustler's trap that may require the suffering of a devastating loss before you understand what happened. Unfortunately, sometimes the best lessons are learning only by experiencing a calamity. The good news is - once such a lesson is learned, you do not easily become a victim in the future (maybe).

Lucky Me

Every once in a while you face a hustler who uses this tactic to throw you off your game. It is designed to be effective over a period of time. He basically trains you to believe that he has the majority of the good luck being handed out by the billiard gods, and you have the majority of the bad luck.

Here is an example of how he gets you thinking that way. Every time he makes a moderately difficult shot, he asserts, in apparent surprise, "I must be lucky today. Usually, I can't make that shot even once in a hundred tries." This shark requires a two-sentence announcement. The first sentence documents his luck, followed by a comment about the difficulty of the shot.

He uses this during several opportunities, such as: makes a good shot, get in good position for the next shot, and leaves you bad when he misses. To make sure you get the message he even comments (several times), "I'd rather be lucky than good." Silly statement on the face of it, but when used multiple times, becomes a strong irritant.

His efforts to appear blessed by the billiard gods are bragged up at every opportunity. He accentuates his positives and accentuates your negatives. His good luck is because of his clean living and high moral standards. Your bad luck is some punishment for an unknown mortal sin. The more you hear about it, the more bothersome it is. Over the match and against your better judgment, you could start believing he might have a point. It's simple brainwashing. The more often you hear something being asserted, the easier it is to think that it is true.

As you start buying into his statements, you make more mistakes. And, if you totally buy into this shark, you realize this is not one of your better days. He can instill within you the feeling or impression that there is no way you can compete against him. After all, he has so much good fortune, and you don't. It is this constant repetition that wears away at your faith in your abilities.

The first few games of the match, he is declaring his good luck. At the middle games, he begins to finesse you. Every time you miss a shot or get a bad leave, he states (in the most innocent of voices), "Don't you wish you had good luck like me?" Or, he says, "I guess you can't be lucky like me." Claiming the good luck is irritating by itself. Declaring you as the victim of bad luck is a double-whack at your focus.

Players who are susceptible to this shark can get so wrapped up in depression that they initiate a search for adult beverages.

Response

Luck does come in streaks. There is a cycle to everything in life, reflected in a continuous series of ups and downs. Think about it as water waves with regular ups and downs. You can look back at your playing experiences and you can identify days when you played better and days that you played worse. It is even noticeable in a series of games. For a period of time, you can't miss. That is followed by a period of time when you can't make even the simplest shot.

Setting aside the sharking, as a smart player, you must have a set of tactics to fit both circumstances. When things go your way, you can open up and take some extra risks. When your shots are less accurate, tuck your horns in and play more cautiously. That's all part and parcel of the game. References to luck, good or bad, cannot change these cycles.

To respond to this trick – be patient. Just as you have experienced ups and down, so does your opponent. When you notice that he is hitting a bad streak – apply the same tactics against him. Declare that he must have irritated the billiard gods with his bragging and they are taking revenge. Do this on every miss and every bad leave.

Also, at every good situation, declare that you are the new favorite of the billiard gods. When you get a good roll, state, "I'd rather be good than lucky." Also use the shorter, "Skill beats luck." Essentially, be an irritant to him as much as he was to you. If he gets pissed off, you have a chance to quickly win a couple of games. This might be enough to either win the match, or at least get you back into competition.

Medical Cane

A pool hustler can take this medical accessory and use it to split off part of your competitive intentions. The basic aluminum medical supply cane makes it obvious that he is suffering some sort of physical mobility limitation.

When played well, he leads you to assume he is a weaker player than he really is. With a cane and a minimum level of acting skills, he can accentuate your sympathetic tendencies. Even a slight effect on your thinking causes you to back off on your game intensity. When you think he's not a threat, why work harder than you have to. Pushovers don't need to be given the full-blown intense "do or die" mentality. You assume he is not the strong player.

He walks around, placing a lot of weight on the cane. This limits the speed in which he maneuvers around the pool table. And of course, he includes appropriate facial and vocal expressions of bravely suffered pain, as appropriate.

The key to sucking you into his trick is to not volunteer any reason for needing this accessory. He even ignores a hesitant effort to inquire about his health. He waits until your curiosity gets the better of your self-discipline.

When you finally directly ask if he is OK to play, he responds, "The doctor insists that I use this thing - something to do with not falling over." With your request for additional details, he now provides an over-abundance of information. He can mention muscle degeneration, ongoing rehabilitation programs, injections of neuron-stimulants, and so on.

This is how he establishes his "weakened" ability to compete. Every time he begins an inning, he wearily reaches over, grabs his cane in one hand and his cue stick in the other. With careful, slow movements, he rises and comes to the table.

There is a slight delay as he stands near the table and analyzes the layout. On getting ready for the shot, he makes a big production about feet positioning. An additional obvious effort is required to get down on the shot.

Sometimes he lays the cane against the side of the table. Other times it is laid across a corner of the table, or even laid on the table. He ensures it doesn't create a foul. It does not interfere with the planned ball paths, and after he strokes the shot, he gets the cane out of the way of any moving balls. Following the shot, he reassembles his body, the cane, and his cue stick. This is repeated for every shot.

An amateur wannabe often gives away this shark attempt in one of two ways – either by over-acting the part or momentarily forgetting to stay in character. An experienced hustler does some dedicated practice in front of a mirror or with a video camera to make sure he gets everything right.

This type of shark doesn't work with any of the canes or walking sticks that are a minor work of art. It's too difficult to convince onlookers about a physical limitation when using a $500 or $1000 walking stick.

Response

As when faced with any player who "apparently" has some sort of handicap or physical limitation, decrepit appearances are always suspect. Think about it. The real game of pool is in the stroke and cue ball control, not how the body is moved around the table.

Don't get sucked into a sympathetic mind set by anyone with physical limitations. Do not feel sorry for anyone when competing on the table. If it was that bad, he should be a railbird, not a competitor. Your basic attitude is to ignore anything except the table, the layout, and the necessary strategies and tactics you must apply to the competition.

You can turn this around and use his trick to actually shark him. Assume an attitude of extreme consideration. Continuously ask him if he is feeling OK. Follow him around the table and stay close by. If he complains, simply say that you want to be there if he happens to collapse.

Constantly ask about his health. "Are you OK?" "Need any help?" "Should I call 911?" What you are looking for in his face is a touch of anger or irritation. That is the point when he is being sharked. You can slow down your courtesies, but continue your concerns for him throughout the match. This should make him an easy win.

Missing Ball

This pool shark combines some delaying tactics with the game of hide and seek thrown in. The hustler only needs to use this a couple times during a match to throw your game focus off kilter. It is rarely the only shark being used against you. But, piled on top of other distractions, it can be one more nail in the coffin of your loss.

All that is required is for him to be in charge of racking the balls for the next game. It doesn't matter whether he is racking for himself or for you. The trick is very simple. As the balls are being assembled in preparation for the start of the game, he leaves one ball off the table. He first moves the balls onto the table and only then brings out the rack.

It is at this moment that he exclaims to everyone – "One of the balls has gone missing."

This initiates a desperate search for the last ball and becomes a major distraction. The competition immediately stops. Anyone who was concentrating on the possible strategies and tactics of the previous games is rudely interrupted. This shark, during the moments it is applied, completely destroys any kind of ongoing thoughtful analysis.

Pocket Table trick

On a pocket table, as the balls are pulled out of the pockets, the hustler leaves one ball in the right or left foot pocket. Every other ball is thrown onto the table to be racked. When he gathers together the balls into the triangle, the mystery of the missing ball is obvious.

Looking confused with a slight frown on his face, he desperately scans the table surface to see if he forgot to include the ball. On this failure, he looks over to you for help. Performing the obligatory assistance to his silent request, you go around and start checking each of the other four pockets on the table. If you don't immediately respond, he stays in place and makes a verbal request for your assistance. And, if you still don't immediately jump up to perform his biding, he reluctantly and with a disappointed look on his face, slowly goes around the table to check the other pockets.

If you do acquiesce and start checking the other pockets, you arise and start looking into or reaching into each pocket. With careful timing, just as you arrive to check the last pocket, he rechecks the pocket where he left the ball, and with an air of surprised embarrassment, pulls the ball out and completes preparation for the game.

There is a minor variation to this trick. He can leave the "missing ball" in the last pocket you would check on going around the table. You would check three pockets, and then discover the ball in the fourth pocket. He can do this by going towards the pocket, removing all but one ball, thereby leaving it for you to find.

Ball Return Table trick

In a ball return table, where all the balls come down to a bucket area at the foot of the table, he removes all of the balls except one. When the missing ball is discovered, he asks you to look into each of the other pockets to see if the ball happens to be stuck in plain sight.

When this verification is unsuccessful, he throws you several balls to roll down the tubes or rails. Only when a ball has been rolled down each of the six pockets does he reach in and "find" the missing ball.

In the same process as above, he is only interested in making you jump around the table pursuing a missing ball that he already knows where it is. Being forced to perform on demand is what distracts.

Response

Only allow the occurrence of a missing ball to happen once. After that, whenever he racks, face away or move away from the table so that you don't see or hear his signal for assistance. The key is to ensure your eyeballs are not within capturing range of his. If you are within earshot to hear his help request, tell him to wait a minute while you fiddle with something. Busy your hands with something and after about 20-30 seconds look up and ask him, "What was it you wanted?" If he looks a little pissed, give yourself an extra point.

Musical Auditions

Are there styles of music that you enjoy? Maybe some rhythm and blues, jazz, classical, doo wop, heavy metal, show tunes, etc. are part of your music library. The stronger your appreciation of music, the greater is the agony suffered from this shark.

The hustler can do things with musical notes and pitch that offends - greatly. There are three variations of how this shark is presented:

- Humming
- Whistling
- Lyric mumbling

The choice of the musical notes is vaguely based on the hustler's personal preference. Whatever is used, the selected so-called musical segment contains a limited repertoire - four to nine notes.

The notes extracted from some song, have just enough similarity to the original song so that the tune can be recognized. The note sequence of the song is mangled to add to the personal irritation you suffer. Your sense of musical appreciation is further aggravated and abused by constant and continuous repetition and with varying volumes.

There are three game situations where this effort of musical notoriety is presented for your appreciation. His variations are offered at seemingly random times, but primarily during:

- His analysis and setup – but quieter and more restrained.
- Your analysis and setup – with more emphasis and volume.

If the hustler also happens to be a champion whistler, he can use that skill when judging the results of each shot. He varies the "tune" according to the shot results. For a pocketed ball, an upbeat set of notes. He emits another positive trill for getting good position. For your good shot and good position, you get a set of 4-6 notes. For his, a set of 10-15 notes.

For miss, he provides a set of melancholy downer notes, something plaintive in a minor key. For your failures, he offers up a set of 8-10 notes, for his failures, 4-6. Remember the purpose is to establish this as part of his playing style and used enough to develop irritated feelings.

Response

There are several ways to respond to the Musical Auditions shark. One of these is to interrupt him in mid-trill and ask, "What song is that? It seems familiar." Make sure you force him to answer. Then say something like, "I love that song."

When/if he uses that same set of notes, join in with your musical contribution. It is important that you do an even worse job of the musical rendition than he is. Feel free to be wildly out of tune and increase the volume. When he stops (probably in amazement at your audacity), continue carrying on with your version. Apply the same style (whistling, humming, or lyrics) as he is using.

Even if the tune is unfamiliar, it doesn't matter. Fake your way through. After you are going solo for a few seconds, stop and ask him how he likes your style. Keep a look of pleasant enjoyment on your face. (There is no need to use sarcasm or evil enjoyment – play this straight.)

Basically, you want to turn his efforts around and present him with the musical distractions, confusions, and irritations. It's easy to override his attempts simply by being more aggressive and louder.

When you notice that he is wincing or frowning, you have beaten him. After that, continue this reverse sharking by using an occasional snatch of music here and there. As needed, include a few encouragements along the way, such as "Come on, all together now." and "You're not keeping up."

If this "playacting" is not within your skills, you can use the "angry" approach. Declare to all who are within earshot of the table that this guy's sharking attempt is one of the most stupid things you have ever experienced in your lifetime of playing pool. At no time is any attempt of strangulation required to counter this shark.

Nervous Enhancement

Everyone experiences some natural and ordinary nervous anticipation at the beginning of an important match. These reactions are the body's natural fight or flight response. Some of the symptoms can include:

- Fast breathing.
- Constriction of the throat.
- Tightness in the chest.
- Sweating and dizziness.
- Difficulty in concentration and focus.
- Hyper-awareness of sounds and movements.

Normally, these symptoms disappear once you get into the competition. But if a hustler recognizes that you are suffering these reactions, he can enhance the intensity of your symptoms to improve his chances of winning. It makes it easier to win the first couple of games to give him an initial short-term advantage.

Therefore, it is to his advantage to "help" stimulate any and all worries that reside within your head. Here are some of his techniques:

- When you make some early mistakes during the first or second game, he states that these errors in playing skills or judgment probably demonstrate that you aren't ready for serious competition.
- Before starting the match, he brags up some of his own past victories and successes in this competition venue.
- If this is a first time at this level, he exaggerates the difficulties and problems – and imply that this might be much more difficult than anything you previously experienced.
- He may dwell on how quickly and easily other newbies to this competition venue were so easily eliminated. He can also describe some episodes when a player choked and lost.

- He can explain how the money winners have all had to play perfect or near-perfect matches, emphasizing the difficulties.

You may not need input from "experienced" competitors to increase your nervous condition. You can do this all by yourself. Here are some of the ways you can self-destruct and sabotage your chances to win:

- Obsessing about losing.

- Remembering past failures.

- Becoming panicky and losing any focus.

Response

If you are self-inflicting your own intimidation, this generally passes after several minutes of play. Put yourself into the game and utilize the same actions and attitude used to beat others. Perform a proper opponent analysis, define his strengths and weaknesses. Craft plans to manage his opportunities. Then execute those plans.

If you are targeted with this shark, there is one emotional reaction that almost immediately washes away any indecision and fear – anger. This is the "fight" response and removes any indecision or confusion in your mind.

This is not the wild reactionary anger of immediately lashing out in response to direct infliction. This is the cold, focused anger of Popeye, when he is finally forced to grab his spinach. It is embodied in his signature quote, "That's all I can stands, and I can't stands no more!"

And, finally, simple experience overcomes this problem. The more times you place yourself in similar competitive situations, the more comfortable you become in handling anything that happens. An attempt at sharking with this trick generally fails before your confidence.

Nit Picking

This sharking trick is a series of small distractions in the disguise of friendly sportsmanship or what could pass as normal playing chatter around the pool table. Nits are little nags about being careful about something important during play. The once-in-a-while reminder in the course of a match could be considered mere courtesy. Multiple unsolicited inputs from your opponent are designed to disturb your intention to win and replace it with low-level irritation. Individually, nits are minor. When presented as a swarm of nits, they are major disturbances to your concentration.

If you are the type of person with low tolerances for interruptions, then you are an excellent victim of this shark. What begins as a minor irritant in the beginning of a match, after several games, they become major intrusions into your game analysis and planning. This is cumulative, so that as you enter the final drive to win the match, just hearing your opponent clear his throat ignites an internal battle to maintain self-control.

Here is a common pool nit, phrased as courteous kindness. "Wait a minute. You should be shooting the 5 ball, not the 11 ball." If he was correct, you are forced to give him credit for good sportsmanship. Not only was a serious playing error avoided (for which you beat yourself up), but you now "owe" him. But it is still a distraction, in spite of the apparent helpful assistance.

In an important competition, there is no reason for him to inform you about the potential foul. He just needs to keep quiet to receive the benefit of the penalty – ball in hand. But, as a sharking effort, he gets to "appear" to be full of good sportsmanship. And of course, his accepted intrusion gives him tacit permission to make comments later in the match.

If you don't provide him an obvious opportunity to be "helpful", it's not difficult to manufacture a reason. His "correction" to a potential foul on your part doesn't even have to be correct. Upon being told that he is wrong, he merely has to apologize – profusely, of course. Nonetheless, he has set the stage for his active participation during your turns at the table.

Regardless of the actual accuracy of his "helpful" behavior (and your internal feelings), you need to respond to his notifications. This means, you are forced to stop playing rhythm, turn to him and politely respond. Because of that redirection of your attention, you now have to restart your preparation routine. And while doing that, he is profusely apologizing for his attempt to be helpful.

After each nit, he keeps quiet for a turn or two. Just when you appear to be getting back into your playing rhythm, he suddenly intrudes again with the same sincere desire to prevent you from making a stupid mistake. Each nit is presented with innocent sincerity. Otherwise, any hint of intentional malice could result in a more dramatic confrontation.

Some examples of nits do not only concern what you are doing. It can also be used for the verification of some playing condition – always when you are at the table, such as, "You're the solids, right?" or some request for clarification. Sometimes the phrase "Are you sure?" is included as soon as you have responded. An expert hustler can even incorporate a third confirmation by momentarily being distracted, seemingly forgetting the answer, and ask again for the answer. The more he works on you, the closer you get to a barely controlled boiling point. If he has successfully hustled you to win the match, you can receive a "final" nit, something like, "Thank you so much for letting me win."

Response

You could handle this effort passively, letting it slide off by simply ignoring anything your opponent says (the deaf response). This tactic only works if you possess excessive patience or are mildly amused that he would seriously think that using such an obvious trick would affect your game.

If you like to become proactive, become the helpful nagger. Continuously provide good advice just as he gets ready to shoot, such as, "Don't forget to chalk." You can also use the "Make sure you stay down on the shot." - which is a really good nag, guaranteed to help your opponent become a homicidal maniac. You can push this too strongly, so do be careful to smile abashedly when he glares in your direction.

Noises

The idea of using noise to distract an opponent during an important or critical shot is an old, old concept. In any critical shot that requires focused attention, any kind of noise distraction can be highly effective in destroying concentration to cause a miss.

Back in the 1920s, the jingling of coins or keys in the pocket was a popular golfing shark. The trick quickly migrated to the billiard room. This and other game changing noises have remained in use to this day. The coin jingling still shows up every once in a while when some kid "discovers" it and finds that it works on his friends. When he finally tries it on a seasoned player, his efforts usually result in public embarrassment.

That specific shark may be old hat, but noises in general are still popular and effective. These do not require line of sight to work. They can be done to you when facing any direction and only need to be loud enough to reach your ears.

There are two types of noise distractions.

- Repeated noise. It can vary in volume and used at varying lengths of time. It can be a foreground (directly intrusive) or background (cumulatively intrusive) noise. It is very effective if you are sensitive to sound.

- Abrupt noise. This is louder and sudden, timed to coincide as closely as possible with your stroke.

Here are a few tricks that can be used against you:

- Knocking and rapping, sometimes in time to any juke box music (or digital music device). If knuckles aren't loud enough, a tool can be used, such as a pen, pocket marker, cell phone, lighter, etc. These ensure the sound penetrates the noise of any ambient background noise, such as a juke box.

- Finger snapping (and toe tapping if the floor is wooden) is common, especially when used with music. Available music (i.e., juke box, MP3 player, etc.) is a good excuse, but not really necessary. Simple humming is enough of a musical accompaniment to apply these noise generators.

- Excessive chalk grinding is feasible – but requires a very quiet environment. When done during perfect silence and with increased pressure, the screeching can be very penetrating. To a billiards purist where the only noticeable sound should be the clicking of balls, this can be bothersome.

- Tip tapping with a cue tool can require active banging to roughen the tip so that it holds chalk better. Excessive use can be effective.

- Stick bouncing is a common way to self-entertain during long waits. The cue is lifted up a few inches and dropped to bounce on its rubber bumper. (Does not work on carpet.)

- Stick falling requires a hard floor (and the use of a house cue). If carpeted, a bunch of house cues have to be knocked over to make enough noise.

- Coughing and sneezing is popular. In an establishment where good manners are a standard of membership, these have to be done using the "stifle" method (turning slightly away and holding one or both hands near your mouth).

Response

If an inexperienced hustler attempts these, you can usually embarrass him into stopping. For example, tell the wannabe hustler, "That old shark has moss growing on it. I haven't seen one of those in years. Where did you dig that up?" Glance over to any railbird and say in a loud voice, "What an amateur."

When you face an experienced trickster, tell him, "Once, but not twice. OK?" If he acknowledges your recognition, you won't be facing other variations on the theme of disquiet. But if he denies any attempt, you have a free-hand opportunity to apply many of the gamesmanship tricks in this book.

This means that you are not restricted in quantity, quality, or volume. The experienced hustler is forced to acknowledge his inability to handle your responses and should be ready to agree to a cease fire.

Odd Habits

A good hustler can take this shark and become very inventive. It is very effective when used in circumstances where there is almost no verbal communications between players. That limitation eliminates most of the sharks that require some sort of conversation. It's hard to declare these as hustling attempts. And many of these might actually be habits, rather than a sharking effort. That doesn't mean the effects (your reduced abilities to compete) don't happen.

Among the variety of the unusual things that have been identified are these examples:

- Wears a baseball cap, frontwards when it is your turn, backwards when it is his turn.

- Wears a cowboy hat, with a one or two pheasant feathers dangling backwards off the brim and which waggles dramatically on every movement.

- Chews on a series of toothpicks the whole match, mutilates them one after the other, and then carefully stacks the remnants in parallel lines.

- Chews on an unlit cigar. When getting ready to make a shot, carefully puts the cigar down with its wet gross-looking end pointed towards you, shoots his turn, and then picks up the cigar and continues his grossness.

- Does a hop or a skip on every other step when walking around the playing area. May throw a twist of the hips in for good measure along with the occasional elbow jutting up to fend off a nearby person or wall.

- Hangs an unlit cigarette out of the side of the mouth. When he's thinking, waggles it up and down and around in alternating circles. When ready to shoot, clenches his lips over the filter.

- Chews gum and then pops it loudly every once in a while, regardless of who is shooting.

- Has a habit of constant stops to peer down at the ground or underneath chairs to look for something. After a few seconds of hunting, straightens up and proceeds.

- Drops several things onto the floor during your turn. Makes a big deal about grunting and groaning while bending over to collect them to make sure you get a good view of his bad side. Very effective with a stack of coins.

- Develops an irregular tic on one cheek. As the cheek lifts in the beginning of the tic, the eye on the same side closes tightly. Only does this when looking at you.

- If he wears dentures, pushes the top or bottom out of his mouth, and then sucks it back in with a slurping sound.

- Walks around with a pair of glasses perched on his head. When ready for a shot, pulls them down and squints at the entire playing area, then pushes them back up.

- Develops the hiccups, which can get worse and louder when it is your turn and less frequent during his turn.

- Pulls a small bottle out of his pocket, opens it and sniffs deeply, smiles hugely with eyes closed, caps the bottle, and puts it back (really contains water, scented or not).

- Brings in a can of Lysol spray, and sprays his seat every time before sitting down.

If you mention anything about his odd habit, he acts embarrassed, maybe walks away for a minute or two while he apparently gets himself under control. He comes back a bit upset and a little angry. He says, "Most people have enough courtesy not to mention my personal handicap to my face." and then goes to his chair to sulk for several minutes. He has to be coaxed back to the game with profuse apologies.

Response

Because these are distractions not involving your direct participation, there is little you can do to stop these being used. He keeps close tabs on your reactions to determine the effectiveness of his effort. Your tightened lips, frowns, or grimaces gladden his heart. For best results, cultivate a tolerance for unusual behavior.

A little more proactive is this effort. Giggle every time he does this. If he stares at you, say, "Can't help it. It's soooo funny." After a few times, move up to guffaws.

Old Geezer

If you are a younger player, this is a trick that an old pool hustler pulls on you. Probably around 60 years of age, he demonstrates the effects of a hard life – or at least a reflection of his ill-spent youth. He has decades of experience. He doesn't really need to hustle anyone, but just does it to maintain his skills in managing minds. If you're in the teens and twenties, he does this just for the fun of it.

As a life-long player, he has been around a long time, seen many things, and learned more than a few lessons about life, especially how it relates to pool. That history includes being on the receiving and giving end of dozens of sharks and hustles of all types and intensities - hundreds of times. There won't be too much that he hasn't already seen and figured out how to use to his advantage. Consider him to be a master gamesman who knows all the tricks, traps, and sharks in this book and several dozens more.

As a long time player and (usually) part-time hustler, he has a handful of hustles and sharks ready for use as the situation may need. With thousands of repetitions, he can swoop and swerve along a dozen responses to anything you do.

One of the standard Old Geezer hustle venues is to determine your level of "innocence". He needs to quickly gauge your past experiences and reactions to obvious and subtle sharks.

The first approach is to use his age. He's looking for the "Really?" response. For example, he says something like, "I have a problem with xxxx <some health problem>." He'll closely monitor your response to this piece of information.

If you say something like, "Really?" or you offer your sympathies – he's got you. If that doesn't' get an adequate reaction from you, he'll fish around until he finds one that you provide the proper reaction.

Once he's got your sympathy, he'll ask that you cut him a little slack. If you reacted to the health ploy, he limps or hobbles or winces when he gets up to shoot. All of these are simply to continue that sympathetic emotional reaction.

Along with these seeming lifestyle restrictions, he'll cheerfully put on a brave front, conversing with a positive attitude. He continues to suppress your competitive mind set. The perfect situation is if he can get you to consider him as an eccentric but nice old uncle. Nobody is dangerous or threatening in any way – until you have to pay up.

His random series of conversational topics softens your game attitude – pushing to make you comfortable and relaxed. All of this is his effort to blunt your game edge. This is all a pleasant game to him – keeping your attention away from the competitive nature of the game.

Response

Ignore it all and concentrate on winning the games. Your public face can give him all the necessary courtesies and respect to be given an aged person. But in your heart and your competitive efforts, treat him as a dangerous opponent. Agree with all that he says. If you can keep him rambling, this keeps him busy while you figure out ways to win the game.

On advantage of playing an Old Geezer is that he uses one or more of the sharks from those long ago times of yester-year. When you know that he is hustling you, you can actually pick up some of those classics and add them to your personal collection.

One response you can use that eventually irritates him (and throw his game off), is the "helpful" ploy. Be overly courteous and condescending. Offer your assistance at every opportunity. Such phrases include, "Need a hand? Let me come over and help." and others can take his attention away from hustling you to defending his own game focus.

Another trick is to stay a little close to him. If he asks why, say, "In case you have trouble getting around; I'm ready to give you a hand." When you can get him to glare at you, you are proactive in affecting his game, instead of being reactive to his efforts.

Partner Divorce

This tactic is used when playing any type of partner's pool game. Your team's two opponents work together in distracting or otherwise affecting your team's abilities to focus on shooting. The concept of a doubles team hustling other team occurs very rarely. Few partnered-up players would have enough common playing experience to work out some of the more sophisticated sharking tricks.

The concept of doubles sharking is not very common. But – when two players are VERY dedicated to winning, this book is filled with tactics they can use. Because few players compete regularly in this format, the results are always in favor of the hustlers.

Given the relative lack of partnered doubles team hustlers does not mean that your team can't get tricked into losing. The efforts are low-class, but can still result in keeping your team from concentrating on the game.

First, the enemy team analyzes you and your partner. They need to identify which of you has the least personal commitment to the partnership. Usually this is the weaker player, easily identified as the recipient of continuous advice. Any indication of resentment or a bit of reluctant participation tells them who their first target is.

Once they select their initial target, they get down to business. For this example, let's assume it is your playmate. The opponent player who shoots before your partner, starts engaging your buddy in conversation. He/she "helpfully" sets up a continuous series of tough shots. Then, when you partner comes to the table, the other opponent player starts commenting about how tough the table is. Advice is freely given – all in a "to help you out" attitude.

Your associate's new-found buddy continues these compliments for a while, and then starts putting you down. He/she designs these uncompliments to help develop the feeling that he is the second class participant in the partnership. The other opponent shooter also agrees and assists in this brain-washing – all done as if you aren't in earshot.

When you make a poor shot – a miss or bad shape – one of the guys expresses appropriate sympathy over your comrade's predicament about being associated with an obvious bar-banger.

All of this is designed to prevent they two of you working closely to help the team win. They intend to drive a wedge between the two of you. If your partner is affected by this psychological attack, he won't put forth his best effort. It also irritates and frustrates you to listen to them.

Response

When you enter a doubles/partners competition, get head-to-head for a few minutes before the match starts. This consulting session is necessary for the two of you to agree upon a common strategy as well as how to handle several common tactical situations. If you are the better shooter, you also need to include some confidence building cheerleading. Working together and synchronizing tactics provides an effective shield against many distractive efforts.

During the battles, do NOT attempt to coach every shot. If you are concerned about how your opponent handles a layout – simply ask, "What do you think is the best option here?" As long as it doesn't totally allow the opposing team to win, let your opponent pick out his own shots.

During the sharking, if your opponents' efforts are affecting your associate's game, you must carefully bring him back into focus. If necessary, take a short break and perform an appropriate pep talk.

If the two of you have experience playing together, you can work on common efforts to counter sharks and maybe even set up a trap or two. For example, attacks on the weaker opponent shark can easily be turned back against the hustlers. Simply apply the same tactics against their weaker shooter. You don't have to expect any success. All you want to do is tie-up their attention spans while the two of you drive towards the win.

Personal Tragedy

Few people are able to compete with deadly intentions against an opponent who has just informed you about a personal tragedy. It's just kind of hard to get into the competitive mood. If you are normally a kind and gentle person, beating up on a suffering human being just is insensitive to the max. In the wide world outside of the pool hall, this is a completely acceptable, even praiseworthy, reaction.

The pool hustler informs you that some tragic event has recently occurred. It is some terrible situation, but something that does not require him to be elsewhere. He made this commitment to play you – and he feels obligated to follow through. And, here he is, being true to his promise. He puts on a brave, even courageous front, bearing up under the weight of his sorrow.

How can you put the whole of your fighting spirit into beating up on someone who is so obviously already beaten down? Such compassion for a fellow pool player takes a lot of your internal competitive fortitude away. It changes your viewpoint of the game and how seriously you can play.

One assumption you adopt is that, because of his problems, he is unable to apply proper focus and attention on the match. You intentionally slack off on your will to win. You no longer have the fierce joyful expectation of a hard-fought battle of wills and skills.

Here is one way the pool hustler can set up the situation. He (hesitantly of course) explains what has happened and the problems this causes in his personal life. Then, he explains that he must complete his commitment to play you. This is where he gives the impression of stolidly soldiering on - a noble spirit, unbowed and unbeaten, head up till the end. He needs only the occasional grimace of internal pain to cross his features (as if momentarily recalling his problem).

Another approach is the "life is beating me up and I'm hurting bad". This requires a constant look of sadness and a mental push to begin his turn at the table, which is also played slowly. He approaches every shot with a morose and glum appearance. Talking is limited to monosyllables.

Here is an example of the two used together. As he shakes your hand, he says in a right tone of voice (but sad look), "Congratulate me. I am now part of the idle class." On a request for clarification, he describes how he just got laid off. He accepts your sympathetic hopeful wishes for a better tomorrow with a wane, "I'm doing my best" smile.

After a few minutes, he drops into the victim phase. He lightly touches on the effects of unemployment - the financial problems, the wife cutting back on expenses, and the depression he is feeling. A few well-heaved sighs help further this facade.

Attempts to raise his spirits are poorly rewarded and barely acknowledged. He wants you to feel guilty about your non-problematical lifestyle. The more convincing he can make this appeal for your compassionate concern, the easier it is for you to slack off and let him win a few games – and the whole match. This kind generosity on your part rewards you with a sober thank you and a sad smile of appreciation for your concern. He has to remember to not appear joyful over the easy win you just placed in his hands.

Response

Most competitive games of pool are not so necessary that they be played when one of the shooters is experiencing personal hardships. Therefore, be suspicious when an opponent presents most types of serious life problems. Think about it. Why would anyone with such difficulties want to get involved in a competitive contest? It would be better for him to stay home and apply an alcoholic sedative.

Rather than back off on your intention to win, consider doing him a favor and win the match as rapidly as possible. If he makes any kind of protest to this seemly callous consideration, tell him straight out, "The sooner I win the match, the quicker you can go home."

With this hustle failing, it's going to be pretty difficult for him to suddenly become very competitive. You should have a decent lead to the win before he shakes off his hustle and tries to get back to a competitive mindset. Spread the word among your pool playing friends so that this guy won't be able to use this trick.

Politics

This shark won't directly affect your game if your political opinions are either in the soft middle or you are politically illiterate. On the other hand, if you have a passionate interest in political discourse and debate, a pool hustler, on knowing this key bit of information, can easily affect your game and concentration.

If you are on either side of the political spectrum with even a mild interest in one philosophy or the other, you can become a victim of this sharking trick.

A savvy pool hustler can apply this shark against you by taking one of two roles. He can play the role of the antagonist, taking a stance and viewpoint that is deeply and thoroughly against your ideas and beliefs. The other role is the protagonist, declaring his support for your opinions and viewpoints.

In the antagonist role, he does his best to become your political enemy. He utters outrageous statements, taunts, and put-downs of various strengths. If you aren't careful, he can wind you up so tight that you even forget that you are in a pool competition.

Whatever you like, he hates. What you hate, he loves. This is extremely effective if you are a flaming socialist-leaning progressive liberal, or a conservative Neanderthal still trying to live in the 1950's.

If you are on the left side of the political spectrum, he starts off with the standard far right patter, "Those god-damn liberals. Always want to take my money and give it to lazy people." Or, "Women shouldn't vote. They're too air-headed to think clearly."

If your assumptions are on the right edges of the spectrum, he complains, "We need the workers, so make all illegal immigrants American citizens. Then they can have gay marriage just like the rest of Americans want. What's the matter with those stupid right-winger morons?"

In the protagonist role, he supports your point of view down to the least and the greatest of your political philosophy. He puts a lot of effort into becoming your best buddy forever. Every idea and concept that you espouse on your side of the fence - he heartily agrees. He is a kindred spirit.

And, of course, when you find such a splendid individual who understands and believes as you do, your opinion of him as a person and friend goes through the roof. Suddenly, the competitive landscape changes from a war zone to a friendly conversation between two good neighbors. You are not playing against a dangerous and tough shooter – you are playing with a good and congenial buddy. He becomes a long-lost brother – which is NOT a good mindset to experience when in a competitive environment.

Whichever approach the hustler uses, his goal is to generate a strong emotional reaction from you. If that happens during a serious competition, you lose.

Response

It's should be a crime to bring the outside world close to a pool table. The standard sub-rule of this exemption means that politics is also a forbidden subject. It is nothing compared to the importance of pool. As far as you are concerned, your entire universe collapses down to the playing area of the pool table. The outside world does not exist. Only the competition and the players matter.

If he does have a chance to get this shark started, there are a few tricks that can throw a monkey wrench or two into his sharking. When he applies the antagonist approach, lead him on with a few pithy insults against him, especially adjectives with "stupid", "idiot", and "crazy" generously distributed.

Then, suddenly and without warning, start agreeing with everything he says. Hug him. Shake his hand. Treat him like a spend-thrift millionaire. This helps confuse him for a while. As quickly as possible, win a few games before he regains his balance.

When he does adjust, switch back to your original position. Lambast him for being a fool and an idiot. A competent gamesman quickly quits, reverting to proper sportsmanlike behavior. An amateur hustler tries to continue, but by the time he figures out what you have done – you have won the match.

Powder & Chalk

To implement this shark, the hustler uses the pool hall's powder and chalk as weapons of mass distraction. This is one of the few efforts that stretch the tolerances of even casual bar-bangers. Most people, observing such behavior, would happily sign a petition to demand a declaration of outlawry. Among groups of regular pool players, the penalty for violating pool hall behavioral standards is exclusion from the group (ostracizing).

This shark is rarely seen in a well-run pool hall. Most of the time, it is observed in use by the most ignorant of bar bangers – not as an intentional shark, but as a simple example of bad parenting.

This sharking trick uses powder (supposed to allow a smooth action of the cue stick over the bridge hand) and chalk (intended to help the cue ball avoid miscuing). The distraction involves the excessive use of powder and chalk during the competition.

When intentionally used as a pool hustle, it destroys a player's game on several levels. The sheer messiness of powdered chalk on the table is very distractive. It's hard to concentrate on a long tough shot when there are several handprints of white powder right beneath your nose.

If you are an inherently neat and tidy person, the scattered powder across the playing area could lead to a nervous breakdown. If you love the Green Game, this desecration generates a major irritation that continues throughout the entire match.

The pool hustler begins this trick by pulling out a small bottle of baby powder from his equipment. He may also have some chalk so old that it disintegrates at a touch.

When ready to begin the competition, he vigorously shakes baby powder into his hand, both front and back. This process also creates a white circle of powder debris around his feet. When he has applied enough (always too much), he vigorously rubs the powder evenly across both hands – which leads to another rain of powder onto the floor. He grabs his stick and vigorously shoves it back and forth through his hand – supposedly to put some of the powder on the stick.

He then walks over to the table, putting the stick down, and creates a loud clap with both hands. This sends out a blizzard of powder that covers half the table and more across the floor. Then, as he finally gets down on a shot, he leaves visible palm prints on the rails and cloth. At every third shot, he renews the powder on his hands. A few turns at the table makes the playing surface look like a paintball war zone.

With his disintegrating chalk, he grinds the tip into the cube with force (and over the table). As the debris falls onto the table, it creates a minor mine field for slow moving balls.

When done drilling the cue tip into the cube, the chalk is placed face down on the rail. This adds more debris on and around the playing area. All of this is designed to provide visual distraction and the destruction of your focus.

Response

Stop this at the first palm outline or chalk cube slam. If you can't personally get a behavior change, appeal to any available higher authority. Look for the opponent's team captain, tournament director, room manager, owner, bouncer, or even other railbirds. (Don't ask any of his friends. They're having too much fun watching their buddy mess up the playing area.) Hopefully, one or more of these individuals can convince him to tone it down. A threat of expulsion or forfeiture of match might help.

In an absolute last resort, rather than attempt to play under such conditions, threaten to quit. If that doesn't lead to a behavior modification, without another word, break your stick down, pack up and go get a drink.

It's not worth putting yourself through this type of playing environment. You certainly cannot enjoy the competition. And don't worry about hurting his feelings. This type of hustler is too callous to be affected by your opinions.

Practical Joker

A practical joke is a humorous prank played on a victim (you), designed to be funny to an audience (the hustling trickster and everyone around you). Your appreciation of the joke is not required and is immaterial to the joke's success. The more public embarrassment, discomfort, or indignity you are exposed to; the more enjoyable it is to the instigator. The experience is usually shocking (sometimes literally) and always surprising. At the very least, the subsequent laughter by the audience over your ridicule is a test of your self-control.

Infrequently, you are faced with an opponent who experimented with practical jokes as a kid and managed to survive to adulthood (probably successfully out-ran his victims). If you dislike being made on the receiving end of a joke or teased in any way, being the butt of your opponent's tricks is painful to your sense of self and dignity.

If he is a life-long trickster, his selection of devices and setups can be extensive. If he is a dilettante, his prop department is smaller. The types of jokes depend on the tools that were packed for the competition. Unless he carries a backpack, this is limited to a selection of a half dozen or so gags.

Each prank was pre-tested, often on co-workers who are guinea pigs for new tricks. The ones he uses are selected to prevent you from developing focus. In a pool hall, the common tricks are the off-weighted crazy cue balls and 8 balls that wobble as they go down the table. Hundreds of practical jokes are available in catalogs and on the web.

Here are just a few:

- Rubber snake or spider.
- Fake poop, vomit.
- Fake wounds, blood.
- Bald head wig.
- Whoopee cushion.
- Hand buzzer.
- Fart spray.

- Breaking glass noisemaker.
- Remote control rat.
- Sweat spray.
- Fake spilled drinks.

Response

Your opponent's intent could be as simple as the misplaced desire to be funny or the malicious intention to apply the maximum possible embarrassment. Regardless, there is not much you can do at the moment of infliction. You may have to force yourself not to take violent action.

If you have some pre-warning of his intentions, there are several things you can do. Your response depends on how pro-active you want to get. At the most dramatic end of the action scale, get wildly upset, then collapse to the ground.

As everyone crowds around, you slowly revive. In a gasping effort, say something about a nervous condition or a weak heart. He should be very much afraid of bothering you again. If you are a pretty good actor, he is almost pathetically anxious to let you win.

For a more passive response, try this. Without a word, walk away from the table and leave the general area. Get a drink or cup of coffee and walk far away to meet and greet friends. After about 10-15 minutes, come back and take a seat in the spectator area.

Act as if nothing happened. Do not inquire as to the status of the game and do not even look at the joker. Whether you let yourself be talked into coming back to the competition is a personal preference.

Propositions

If you are a younger player, you are more susceptible to this hustling trick. As a general rule, less aged shooters seem to be willing to take larger chances on shots that old-timers are wise enough to stay away from.

In a situation where a long-time player would seriously consider defensive options, the youngster is happy to take a flyer if he thinks he has even a small chance to pull it off.

The pool hustler must first determine if you are vulnerable to proposition bets and challenges. Early in the game, he throws a little test at you.

On a tough shot where you should play cautiously, he offers, "I'll give you a buck if you can make it." If you try it, he knows you are a prime target for this distraction. It doesn't matter if you succeed or not.

If you refuse, he prompts for a rationale. If you respond with a sensible answer, like, "That's beyond my ability." or another intelligent remark, he knows you are a thinking player. He might still offer a proposition, but mainly for its temporary distractive value as you consider and reject the offer.

Here are a few circumstances where this can be applied:

- At a key shot in the game, that if successful would win the game.

- The difficult but not impossible shot.

- Just past the mid-game point on an important game.

- On a very low percentage shot, for the fun of it.

He can make the proposition as simple as an even up offer, or handicap the offer to make it more attractive. But it is not the size of the bet as much as the distraction it causes.

4. Any rhythm you might have had is now disrupted.

5. You must stop and listen to his proposition.

6. You evaluate the possibilities.

7. You respond - yes or no.

8. If yes, you have the new pressure of the bet.

9. If no, you must refocus your attention.

If you take the bet, it doesn't matter when you win it or not. He accomplished the original intent - taken your attention off the competition – from which it takes some time to recover.

Response

There is not much you can do to stop your opponent from throwing out a proposition. It is a blatant effort to interrupt your rhythm. If you have been exposed to proposition bets before, it is a simple process to immediately wave him off and continue your shot.

This response diminishes the effort as no more distractive than any background conversation or the jukebox suddenly starting up.

If unfamiliar with proposition bets, you probably allow him to make his proposal. Your best option is always refusal, no matter how interesting the offer. Keep in mind – the more tempting the proposition, the more guaranteed you are to reduce your quantity of ready cash. To get back to the game, apply a couple of internal calming routines as you get back to the game.

Because your opponent made the offer, he has opened the door for you to present your own propositions during his turn at the table even while he is getting ready to shoot. When you see a similarly difficult position facing him - make your offer. Time it just as he has made one or two practice strokes.

It is always a bit disconcerting to a pool hustler when his own tricks are immediately recognized and used against him. He might test you with another shark, but the distractive affects is greatly diminished.

Put-downs

Unlike insults where your opponent makes no bones about pushing your ego into the mud, this sharking effort pretends to have a veneer of good sportsmanship. The distractions are always presented as a two-part effort. The first part is a meaningless compliment. The second part is the slanderous statement. If you consider the opinions of others to be reality, this shark is very effective in helping you lose the match.

The subject matter of these observations covers the entire gamut of your playing skills. His contributions of opinions run the gamut from your pre-shot routine, cue ball control, intentions, strokes, consequences, and your ability to apply intelligent thinking to each shot. Anything you do is fair game for his observations and comments, so long as it can divert your focus, even slightly.

Every comment he utters utilizes a two-part statement. First is the obligatory compliment apparently in the spirit of good sportsmanship. This is followed by the dig, jab, or poke at your self-esteem. Here are a few examples:

* That was good. And, you almost got position too.

* Congratulations on that tough shot. I guess luck is more important than skill.

* Nice shot. Too bad you couldn't get the cue ball into a decent position.

* Good try. But it looks like you can't run out from here.

* Good run. It looked good right up until you screwed up.

* I'm impressed with the shot. But not your control.

To check your sensitivity level, he throws out a couple of investigatory jabs, and then closely watches your reactions. Any twitch, frown, or grimace encourages him.

The intensity increases as the game progresses. By the end-game, the level depends on whether he is winning or losing. If winning, he reverts to the milder version. If losing, he is more aggressive and may abandon the veneer of sportsmanship and go to straight insults.

Response

This won't work if you don't care what anyone says about you in specific or in general. And when you can't be affected in this way, your opponent is wasting his time. Because of your stable self-confidence, his offensive remarks cannot be taken as a personal affront to your abilities.

You can use this as a motivation to play with greater focus. There is a certain amount of self-satisfaction in using this shark attempt as a self-motivator. Regardless, be deliberate in performing all the necessary table analysis and shot selection. Perform all of the proper routines through to the execution.

You can apply the silent treatment, ignoring anything and everything your opponent may say or do. Simply withdraw yourself from all communication with your opponent. When your opponent shoots, turn away from the playing area. Absolutely do not allow any eye contact. Force him to tell you to you when it is your turn to shoot.

If you can handle a more aggressive approach, get into an exchange battle. Play the same schoolyard games you experienced in elementary school. Extra points if you can out-insult him to silence.

This distracts both of you during this process. The trick to quick recovery of your focus is that you intentionally initiated the insults. That makes it a lot easier to regain focus and intention. While he is stilling feeling the reaction to your efforts, you have a chance to pick up a game or two.

There is still the option to make a direct request to stop being childish. This has to be delivered in a parental tone of voice. This can be effective when the request is made in front of a group of railbirds.

Rules Expert

The rules committee members for pool and billiards players work very hard to ensure clarity and explicit explanations for the rules of competition. Even so, there are always many areas where interpretations can be applied. It's the Clinton excuse, "It depends on what the meaning of the word 'is' is." This area is ripe for abuse by the pool hustler. It is the ongoing, ready-to-dispute attitude of nit-picking and quibbling is what makes this sharking trick work.

The hustler must invest a significant amount of preparation and study into every set of rules at the local, national, and international level. Being a gamesman, the intricacies of rules have a natural fascination. He is greatly involved with studying the whole concepts, intentions, down through the microscopic levels. (This fascination of micro definitions is why some people become lawyers – and then politicians.)

There are levels of rules expertise qualities. At the low end, you find the dilettante dabbler. This person attempts to appear to be an expert rules master. But because he is a dilettante, he won't have put in the necessary study time. At this level, the wannabe expert happily misinterprets the rules and gets many of them just plain wrong.

He can even be capable of making up rules on the spot. He covers up his ignorance and half-knowledge by increasing the strength of his vehement declarations of expertise. He can get downright loud when his rulings are challenged (the louder, the more unsure he is about the truth of his judgments).

In action, the hustler's eagle eye closely watches your every movement starting when you come into the playing area. He pays close attention to all of your actions. Every body movement, shift and adjustment is judged against every possible interpretation of the game rules.

Another thing he has to verify if whether you are knowledgeable about all the rules. This can be verified with a few test questions, such as, "Are we playing APA or BCA rules?" If you express some knowledge, he may probe further – or assume you have a layman's knowledge.

From that basis, he starts closely monitoring your every action from racking to shooting. On your first violation (or his perceived observation of violation), he throws himself into the declaration of your "error" – with great enthusiasm. Much depends on the seeming certainty of his knowledge.

His first exuberance is designed to catch you unawares. It is designed to disrupt your rhythm and has the bonus of completely removing your attention on the game to his complaint. He might be right or wrong – it really doesn't matter.

If you argue about it and somehow win, you return to the game feeling irritated and upset - not a good mind-set for competitive situations. If this is followed by poor playing, you get even further upset with yourself. Even if he is wrong and you prove it, that doesn't change the affect he has made on your playing attitude.

After that first massive distraction, he probably implements the "constant reminder" tactic. Whenever you are setting up for a shot, he "helpfully" reminds you of a potential rule violation that you must be careful not to commit. This constant intrusion into your attention on playing the game is a major distraction to your playing rhythm. All of this benefits him and hurts you.

Response

When you come across such an opponent, every time he calls out the penalty, insist that he get out the rule book and show you the exact wording. Do this even when you know you have committed the violation. It never hurts to keep him concentrating on looking up rules instead of playing his best game.

If he declares a violation you are unfamiliar with, force him through the proof process. You might learn something. Use him to educate yourself about some of the more obscure rulings. You might pick up a tip or two to use against future competitors.

If he doesn't have a rule book, dramatically express shock and dismay. Ask him, "How can you call a foul if you don't even have the rules with you? What's the matter with you?" Mock him for the rest of the match. Every once in a while, catch his eye and sadly shake your head.

Self-inflicted Delusions

This is one of the easiest sharks that a pool hustler can use against you – your own false ideology, constructed on a delusional belief in competency.

In competitions around the world, there are players who are intellectually dishonest about their skills and capabilities. This personal assumption is based on the player's belief that his true skill level was established during the one competition in the past (recent or decades ago) when everything went right and all was successful. That was a glorious day when nothing went wrong.

Your assumption of a skill level and competence that cannot be factually proven is all the hustler needs to know. All he needs to do is encourage you to play beyond your abilities and basically hustle yourself into losing. If you suffer from this potential for over-estimation, then almost every game and match cannot demonstrate that previous competence. All the hustler needs to do is observe the types of shots you attempt. If he observes that reality does not intrude upon your assumptions, he's got an easy mark.

This is how you apply this self-imposed fantasy to your competitive efforts. Every loss is not your fault – but only the consequences of bad luck. This presumption of proficiency has become your basic assumption. And you can't understand why there is such a significant break between that fantasy and the reality of your current competitive skills.

With the true dedication of the slightly insane, you refuse to learn from experience. That past triumph is continuously held up as the truth, the whole truth, and nothing but the truth - actual demonstrable circumstances be damned.

The hustler loves players with these unrealistic expectations. All he needs to do is watch groups of players compete. He watches players (like yourself) miss a tough shot – and then moan and groan that it should have been easy. Mentally, he is already calculating how much he can take you for.

These false-expectations players actually believe many low percentage shots are within their skill level. They always have that rare winning experience quite vividly implanted into their brain. Any single unexpected success is claimed to be proof of his amazing skills.

So, whenever a shot attempt fails (no matter how simple, or complex), your friends and opponents must listen to you complain aloud or mutter vile deprecations under your breath. Statements like "Should have had that." and "Just once I'd like to play my regular game.", and "Damn. That was not a difficult shot." become your normal conversational contributions and the hustler to mark you for future slaughter.

Of course, not only are you living in a fool's paradise, you are also telling every opponent exactly what types of shorts are difficult for you to make. You are letting everyone know that you have another weakness to be exploited. Any opponent who intelligently analyzes your abilities has just been handed a tool to easily win every match.

Response

One of the most basic realities of intelligent competition is this little bit of Shakespearean advice, "To thine own self be true." Basically, this says that you are much better off keeping your expectations based in reality.

If you can make tactical decisions on a frank appraisal of your chances for success, your chances of pocketing balls and moving the cue ball around the table for the next shot become much more realistic.

If reading this sharking trick awakens some awareness that you take lots of trips to fantasyland, you can throw some cold water on your imagination and make more intelligent playing decisions.

This is not to say that there are times when you really become a super competent shooter. When that happens, allow your brain and muscles to freely guide you to winning the match. But when you notice that edge becoming dull, immediately drop your level of expectations and pull yourself out of the fantasy and into the real world.

Self-doubt

If introspective by nature, you are a careful and thoughtful pool player. You understand the importance of setting up properly for each shot and that fundamentals (stance, setup, and stroke are necessary to playing a good game. As a thinking pool player, you probably have a small library of instructional material that has proven to be effective and helpful. The occasional lessons from pool instructors with good reputations have thoroughly established in your mind the important values of constant and consistent routines. You are a "thinking" player.

Along comes this pool hustler – all nice words and friendly attitude. He gets to playing with you and starts laying the groundwork to make you more vulnerable to sharking tricks. And because your game is based on your true skills and abilities, his normally effective distractions and confusions don't work on you.

An experienced gamesman, knowledgeable in all of the tricks of hustling is not put off by your seeming invulnerabilities. When the first sets of "standard" tricks fail to get results, he easily discards them. This shark is often saved as the back-up hustle – the intentional and thorough destruction of your self-confidence.

The sophisticated pool hustler is also a dedicated billiards enthusiast. He is knowledgeable about the whole of the game (history, famous shooters, more than a nodding acquaintance with the main instructional books, and the culture).

Once he has established his "credentials" as an experienced and thoughtful player himself, he can begin his dirty work – the complete disintegration of your trustworthy shooting and playing routines.

The simplest and most effective approach is simply getting you to focus your attention on some of your routines that have been under your control for years.

All he needs to begin is to get you to agree that he is knowledgeable enough to provide valid suggestions and recommendations. This is not something that can be done easily – since you have a good stable foundation. His credibility is established over two or three games. But once he is "under the hood" of your fundamentals (with your tacit approval), you are ready to be his victim.

For example, it might be his strong recommendation to make a minor change in foot placement. By introducing one small change in your routine, he has given you a new set of tasks – on each and every shot, you have to consciously make the recommended physical adjustment.

This is not to say that his advice is exactly correct and actually necessary to improve your shooting. In fact, the more true and valid his recommendations are, the more thoroughly your adjustments mess with your routines. Here are some situations where he can force you to "re-think" a routine:

- How far back you move a hand or foot before execution.
- How far your follow through goes.
- The various back and forth distances for practice shots.
- Where your feet are placed.
- Your body balance.
- The set and angles of your shoulders or hips or knees.

Basically, he is pulling your mind into one of those mental tricks your playmates used to mess up your hopscotching skills, the trick known as "Don't think about purple elephants."

Response

A person who thinks too much requires the occasional reality check. After all, why would someone you are betting some amount of money (or prestige) be interested in improving your game? If your playing is that bad, he should be pitching his special 12-hour correctional shooting analysis and tune-up course at a one-time price of $239.

Therefore, all ideas, suggestions, recommendations, and/or assistance offered by an opponent deserve discussion AFTER the competition, not during. If you hold to this, a smart hustler recognizes when his tricks are discovered and move on to some other tactical tricks.

Sex Appeal

In pool halls across the planet, most (about 60-65%) of the players are of the male gender. There is always the normal competitive spirit that occurs between two opponents. When the dynamics of opposite sexed players is added, it becomes much easier to be a railbird rather than the close competitive environment of the pool table.

A female drop-dead gorgeous hustler with curvy body parts almost falling out of barely adequate restraints (and the male equivalent) are more an adolescent's fantasy than any chance of actually occurring.

Let's pull back everyone's imagination and ground the information about this sharking trick in some reality. Most women apply a certain amount of femininity to the match. And that has a greater or lesser impact, based on the other player's experience with the opposite sex.

It is also rare to find a well-trained female gamesman (gameswoman). They are out there but are well camouflaged. These experts flirt through the billiard gods universe leaving no ripples and very little evidence of their existence. Fortunately for so many male players, gameswomen tend to limit their talents to the general playfulness of social environments and do not apply their skills with the ruthlessness so often seen by male hustlers.

Nonetheless, any competent female player (B level or higher) can easily change the odds of winning, just as a matter of normal competition. Young guys with little experience interacting with women are much more susceptible, but even old geezers are not above being affected by an innocent-appearing smile.

Any female pool player, who applies her natural advantages as tools in the battle of the sexes, can be distracting on multiple levels. Even dialed down for public consumption, the guy is constantly aware of her presence, cutting back the quality of his game focus. Age and beauty are actually immaterial. It is the manners and attitude that determine the effectiveness.

Some of the tools women use around the pool table includes:

- Clothes (sweaters, pants, tops, shorts, dresses – both long and short, etc.
- High heels
- Earrings & necklaces
- Perfume
- Hair styles

And, of course, there are the delivery mechanisms:

- Walking
- Talking
- Smiling
- Existing

A gameswoman carefully observes your reactions. When the areas of your attention are identified, additional efforts continuously present the most effective distraction.

Response

There is not going to be much you can do to stop a skilled gameswoman from using her tools and tricks. Guys are pretty much victims in the battles between the sexes.

Attempts to become a misogynist (woman-hater) for the duration of the match are usually short-circuited by a smile or pleasant compliment.

The best thing you can do is concentrate on winning as quickly as possible. Stay as far away from her as the playing area allows. Concentrate your attention on the pool table and what is happening there. Avoid eye contact, keep communications minimized, and pay attention to the game. After the competition, you can return to being a normal person.

Shark Yourself

You can play for 50 years against all types of pool players with skills great and small. Each and every one of these opponents owns a variety of sharks of varying effectiveness. Many of these are of the minor variety, relatively benign in effort, intention, and application. Watch anyone play pool for half an hour and you can spot a minimum of three sharks. Some people, when their sharks are identified, are surprised. Generally, these relatively minor sharking tricks have become part of his playing routine.

Ask any 10 players if they regularly shark, five deny it with righteous indignation, four blushingly admit to the occasional sin, and the last is forthright in declaring he has an addiction to mind games.

Even counting all of these in the total number of distractions that have been directed at you throughout your playing career; that is a fraction of the sharks you played against yourself! This is an astonishing truth that few want to face and address.

Here is a very short list of some of those ways you confuse yourself.

- Saying, "I hope I don't miss, or look stupid, or scratch."
- Someone maybe, might have, could have sharked you.
- Someone moved, or stopped.
- Someone laughed, or cried.
- Someone said something, or didn't.
- Shirt is too tight, or too loose.
- Shoe laces are loose, or too tight.
- Pants crotch digs in, or doesn't.
- Belt too tight, or loose.
- Music too loud, or not playing.
- Forgot to splash on some cologne, or put on too much.
- Someone turned away, or turned the other way.
- Someone dropped something, or picked it up.

- You didn't drink enough, or too much.
- Ate too much, or not enough.
- Room is too hot, or too cold.
- You have a personal problem, or maybe two.
- In itch here, or there, or there.
- A pretty girl, or another pretty girl.
- Poor execution or equipment.
- and so on and on and on.

There are thousands of things that can bother you, from the simple to the complex, from the personal to the impersonal. With the right frame of mind, you can be distracted by gravity.

Response

Physical exercise can help remove some of these distractions by dulling the too-bright intensity of your mind. With less "awareness" of everything, you can get back to an ordinary playing attitude. Try doing one or more of the following (out back if possible - don't want to get people talking):

- 20 jumping jacks (make sure you have room).
- 20 deep knee bends (in the bathroom, the handicapped stall support bar is very helpful).
- 3-5 minutes of jogging in place (quietly).
- Brisk walk around the block (make sure the neighborhood is safe).

Another way is to take a moment to count your blessings, starting with the fact that you are alive and mobile. Think for a moment on what your life would be like if you had the problems that other people have mentioned. Once you can trivialize your original distractions, you can get on with your pool game using a more vitalized point of view.

Shockers

A shocker shark is any activity designed to destroy your game focus and make it difficult to recover any ability to play effectively. It does this with an action that is a complete surprise. It can be a shock to your sensibilities or to your nervous system. It can even go so far as to be a dangerous threat to life and limb. At its more intense levels, this is a gross violation of the spirit and idea of sports. The lesser shockers often fall within the spectrum of juvenile horseplay.

There are always a few pool players with a poorly developed sense of propriety that are willing to try this. If you are a nervous person, affected by sudden unexpected movements or sounds, this is one of the tricks that a hustler uses against you. A socially inept person can be looking for a bit of fun through by executing a surprise attack – expecting to achieve an early victory based on the shattered remnants of your concentration.

Unless you have some experience of exposure to a great variety of noises and surprises, your mind generally shuts down and your hind-brain is suddenly left in charge. When your fight or flight response is triggered, your body prepares to act. This can generate an embarrassing reaction ranging from diving for cover while emitting a shrill scream to the frozen immobility of a possum. Besides the immediate reaction, the entire body tenses up as it is flooded with adrenalin and endorphins - not a good thing for a pool player who depends on a quiet playing environment.

Shockers have varying degrees of intensity and affect people differently. Here are some various types:

- The most extreme shockers are the very loud dangerous noises, including explosions and rending metal. The sheer volume indicates some kind of life-threat is extremely close and is seriously dangerous.

- Just below this are the sudden sharp noises that occur nearby when least expected. Examples are the firing off a starter's pistol, lighting off a fire cracker, the blare of a juke box after several moments of quiet, or knocking down a rack of sticks. While the reaction is not the desperate scramble to save your life, it can include jumping away from the immediate area or a crouching drop to the floor.

- Below this, are sudden movements and actions that are most effective when seen with peripheral vision. It could be someone hitting you on your blind side, or a sneak poke of a body part. It can also be a social surprise, such as the exposure of a normally covered part of the anatomy.

Response

You can't really call a player who uses any of the shocker variations – a pool hustler. It is most often the teenage youths who think this is a witty way to play pool. Such individuals are also loud, announcing their existence across the width of the pool room.

This does not mean that a shocker can be applied by a skilled hustler. It is done once during a match – carefully timed. The use of a shocker MUST appear to be accidental, such a letting a cue fall to a hardwood floor. If you attempt to split your attention between the shot and his possible actions, he doesn't even have to actually use a shocker. Just the implied assumption that it could happen would be efficient enough to satisfy the hustler.

Alternately, use such an attempt to "explode" at the guy. Shout, yell, insult at a loud volume to intimidate him. Most hustlers like to be sneaky, but if you make him the center of your anger, he can usually be cowed into submission – not only for this match, but all future matches the two of you play. Extra points if you can get people to eyeball him with suspicion.

Another pro-active approach to a sudden noise is faking a faint or even a heart attack. Such drama also frightens him away from future use.

If you were affected by the trick, take a short bathroom break. Do a couple quick toe-touches, windmills, jumping jacks to blow off the excess energy. Then go back to the table with your strongest, most focused attention to win.

Slow Racker

This is a delaying sharking trick. Basically, by stretching out the simple process of racking the balls for a game, the pool hustler wants you to also run out of patience.

As of this writing, no rules committee has declared a mandatory time limit spent racking the balls. This tactic works whether his is racking for your break, or when he is racking for his break. All he needs to do is push your tolerance.

If you ask why the delay, he declares with a true self-righteous voice that he wants to provide the "perfect" rack. During this entire process, the hustler is intently focused on doing exactly that - regardless of the imperfection of the table, balls, cloth, and spot.

Since he is racking, he decides what his minimum standards are. At the least it includes all balls touching, head ball exactly centered on the foot spot, and the balls perfectly aligned. Anything less is abhorrent to his personal quality standards.

It starts when the balls are collected and rolled down to the foot of the table. Instead of sweeping all the balls into the triangle with a quick swoop, he picks each one up and carefully drop it into a position in the triangle. Immediately following the ball placements, he moves the balls around for another test of your patience.

When a table has seen a lot of action, many incidental activities have occurred to make playing conditions less than perfect. That includes sprays of chalk from tips, cloth burns from balls hit at high speeds, indents from bouncing balls, and general use abuse.

All of this wear and tear makes it difficult to keep any of the balls in the rack in touch with each other. Putting the rack of balls into position, then lifting the rack often finds several balls drifting away from each other like reverse magnets. Yet, everyone else that racks balls for their competitors can usually do so in less than 30 seconds.

There he is, pushing the rack up to the spot, lifting it slightly to observe a ball shift, then putting it down and moving the balls again. He tries fiddling with the balls, pushing each this way and that to try to get them to stay in place.

The rack is pulled down, sideways, back up, and re-attempted. This is followed by shaking it hard, moving the balls around, then thrusting them forward in a sudden jerk. Over and over and over, with inhuman patience he attempts to be successful. Three minutes later, he's still going at it.

On each variation attempted, he glances up at you, displaying a helpless look of resignation. FINALLY, if you haven't already angrily taken over the rack, he adds insult to injury. He looks up at you and asks, in all sincerity, "Do you want to inspect the rack?" If you refuse, he begs for your inspection. "Please, I want this to be as perfect as possible." As you grudgingly come down to look, he asks, "Is this OK? I can try again."

Response

Once you have identified this trick as an intentional shark, you can relax. Instead of impatiently waiting at the head of the table, go back to your chair, kick back and entertain yourself with cue maintenance activities or conversations with buddies. You can take the time to get a drink or snack.

His attempt to irritate requires an audience of you. There is a strong possibility that if he sees his efforts don't work, he just finishes the rack and allows the game to proceed routinely.

If you want to be a bit pro-active, let him finish the rack. Only then do you rise from your chair and saunter over to inspect the rack. Declare your dissatisfaction and request another effort. Return to your chair and continue relaxing.

Another action option is to wait for the balls to be sent down to the foot of the table and he has gotten the rack out. Then rudely push him aside and do it yourself. While he gapes at you in astonishment, smile pleasantly and get the game started.

Slow Shooter

This is another delaying shark that is often observed in pool. To implement this effort, the hustler simply slows down his basic shooting routine. Used by a master gamesman, it becomes less a game of pool and more of a game of Patience. This tactic stretches out the amount of time that he is in control of the table – which extends the time you spend sitting down.

A casual (amateur) hustler may have accidently discovered this technique; either used against him or watched it being done against a friend. The trick and the results can be fairly obvious to an observer. Over time, he uses this trick primarily as a technique to slow down an opponent's run of good luck. He would use it in the same way a football time-out is called when the opponent's offense (or defense) seems to be tougher than usual.

An experienced hustler has many options. He can integrate the process into his routine as a default shooting style against a particularly vulnerable (impatient) opponent. He can utilize it constantly, although his normal competitors easily recognize the shark and take mental preparation steps to counter. Even a natural style, against new opponents, it can be very effective. As with the amateur, it can be a routine response to a player shooting the lights out.

This tactic becomes VERY dangerous when applied during end-games and when the match is very close (i.e., hill-hill). He wants to modify your state of mind from the deadly focus of a predator to the irritated (or even furious) result of impatience.

Here is the basic slow shooter routine:

1. He lays the tip of his cue stick behind the cue ball to track the shooting line. (Waits several seconds.)

2. The feet are then positioned, very carefully. First, the back foot is placed. In slow motion, the front foot is moved. Slowly, he bends down over the stick. (This can take up to 20-30 seconds).

3. Next the bridge hand is set up – maybe switching from open to several varieties of closed bridges.

4. Adjusting the bridge hand height, he experiments with draw and follow. (Another 15 seconds gone.)

5. Now the eyeballs switch back and forth from cue ball to object ball.

6. Several practice strokes are made – all in slow motion.

7. If he wants to be particularly irritating, this is when he stands up and repeats.

8. Eventually the shot gets shot, after which he seems frozen in place on the table (apparently cogitating the results.

9. If unsuccessful, he can spend another 10 seconds leaving the table. If successful, you are forced through reruns.

Any steps can be made into a mini-movie production about careful setup. The practice strokes could be extended out to 20+. A full-blown effort could easily turn one shot into a three to five minute marathon.

If he has a talent for torture, he can first setup on the wrong ball to make you hope for a momentary lapse in judgment. Then, as if realizing his mistake, gets up and moves to set up on the correct shot – causing another anticipated hope to be dashed to the floor.

Response

Of course, he has to carefully judge your controlled patience. This shark has been known to backfire and result in much pain to the hustler.

Demanding he stop this simply proves his efforts are fruitful. In tournament play, invoke Rule 19 of the World Pool-Billiard Association Rules and demand a shot clock. In a personal competition, you need to take another path.

First, chose not to be temperamental. Instead, use the time to study the layouts. Consider the many dozens of shooting options available, both offensively and defensively. Mentally play these options to evaluate their feasibility.

By attempting to use this tactic on you, he has given you an excellent opportunity to play with greater intelligence. You would be surprised how many clever ideas your mind can generate.

Smoking

There are still a few jurisdictions and countries where smoking in a public place (pool halls, bars with pool tables, etc.) is not strictly prohibited (or totally ignored). These lonely locations are usually in areas where tobacco has not been super-regulated. If you play in pool halls where smoking is still allowed, watch out for this shark attempt. This requires a relatively limited air space with limited air flow. A small bar with a beat-up pool table would be an excellent venue for this effort. It does not work in outdoor situations.

The pool hustler doesn't necessarily need to have a tobacco habit, but does need a relatively high tolerance for tobacco smoke. This is effective when you don't smoke. It is also effective if you do smoke but have a lower tolerance level.

When the competition begins, the pool hustler engages his tobacco weapon. Usually, it is a cigar or even a pipe. Either one does not require inhaling the smoke.

The odor has to be offensive and even more so when concentrated in a small area. For ease of building volume and density, the pipe is more favored. The cigar has to be cheap (and smell it). No need to waste a good cigar on a sharking effort. There are several awful smelling pipe tobaccos out there.

The density of the smoke is an important aspect. It should be thick enough so that players need to peer through the smoke. Anything less does not achieve the maximum distraction. The density is maintained by the continued presence of smoldering cigars (oftentimes, several are used) in various ash trays. And of course, a few quick puffs a couple minutes apart are also effective.

During this "tobacco smoke" attack, care is taken to ensure that smoke clouds are maintained over your chosen chair. Every time he walks around the table, he stops to consider the table, casually issuing multiple puffs in your direction to add or renew the density. Anytime he is absent from your area, the clouds start dissipating, requiring his continuous walks around the table.

An experienced hustler takes care not to asphyxiate himself. During his shots, he sits in his chair for a few minutes to allow air currents to clear the air a bit. You won't see him puffing and huffing when it is his turn.

Parts of his calculations include reducing the oxygen flow to your brain. If he can do that, he cripples some of your ability to develop clever shooting solutions. His trick is additionally effective when you are bothered by the tobacco odors. For some people, sensitive to tobacco smoke, these clouds also generate a sore throat and tearing eyes.

Response

If you are unable to stand presence of tobacco smoke in your atmosphere, you should find another playing location with a more intolerant view of smoking. At least, find a place with much larger square footage to spread the smoke out.

If caught up in this enclosed tight space, the first thing to do is go around and put out every smoldering tobacco product out. For cigarettes and cigars, dropping them into a glass of liquid (water or beer) takes them out of commission and destroys their reusability. Explain this off as a reaction to a near-death experience suffered years ago. (The excuse doesn't have to be true, just reasonable.)

If you know the pool room is smoke-filled, bring in one of those cheap Oriental folding paper fans. One of those little battery-powered air movers also works. When it's your turn, make a production out of fanning away the air above and around the table. Intentionally direct the air flow towards your opponent. Only then start your inning at the table.

Another option is the "fresh air break". Take one everyone h shoots and then stay out for at least a couple minutes. You can for every inning, take a break. Then, take another break after you make two or three balls and while it is still your turn. As a last resort, pull the nuclear option - refuse to play as long as any lit tobacco product is within 20 feet of the table.

Stand By Me

This is a simple hustler's trick. This distraction tactic is most effective when there isn't a lot of room around the pool table. This means that there are not always designated chairs for the players.

This shark can be used in any informal competitions, such as team matches, local tournaments, and any playing areas that have to crowd a lot of players onto the tables. It cannot be applied during formal competitions where players have designated seats in which to wait while the other shooter plays his inning.

The hustler sets the "tone" for the shark by acting with apparent good sportsmanship – seemingly to ensure that he does not interfere with your shooting.

There are many ways to make this work to his advantage. Such movements most often occur after he has determined your next shot. In the process of getting out of your way, he always takes the longest route around the table. This ensures he spends the longest amount of time in front of you.

He can stop slightly to one side of your aiming line, and freeze into a motionless statue. And just as you are making your stroke, he makes a slight movement in one direction or the other. He can also "seemingly" become aware that he is in front of your shot, and then scurry quickly to the side – while apologizing profusely for being in front of you.

As he moves around the table to avoid being a distraction, the direction tends to be the one that pass you on the same side of the table. At the least, his moving into and through your personal comfort zone ensures you are momentarily distracted. This helps tatter your focus and concentration.

When he doesn't want to directly push past you, he can take the long way around the pool table – so that he has to travel 3/4 around to get into a location that shouldn't distract you. And of course, he does this as you are getting down on the shot.

A variation of the "Stand by Me" hustle involves him spending the majority of his "not-moving" time on the edge of your peripheral vision. Most of this table circumventing is on your shooting side.

If you shoot right-handed, he stops moving on your right side. As he moves around to keep out of your way, he occasionally asks, "Is this OK? I'm not in your way?" This is to make sure you don't forget him while you are focused on your game.

Another tactic is to carefully ensure that he always is behind you on your shot. Even out of sight, he can make sure to impinge on your concentration. In a cramped playing area, he may intentionally jostle somebody – then, apologize to that person while you are trying to concentrate.

He may make a noise, shift a table or chair out of the way, or even have a cough. If you do turn to take a look, he makes smiles or laughs embarrassingly and says an appropriate, "Sorry.".

If you call him on it, he is very profuse about his apologies. He may even behave for a short time. A few turns later, he gently starts up again.

Response

An amateur hustler over does this. When you recognize this as an intentional distraction, tell him to stop being so stupid – loudly. In a crowded playing environment, you might even get a few laughs from the railbirds.

If done of an experienced hustler, it's hard to actually identify this. This is because the shark is only used during critical shots. When you know this type of hustle can be done, it is easy to recognize.

An immediate and very direct action is needed to stop this. Get his attention and say, "When you are shooting, I will stand there (point to the area). When I am shooting, you can stand over there (point to the area). OK?"

Usually, this should do the trick. At least it stops this shark. It doesn't mean that he won't try something else.

Stick Whisperer

This is a distraction effort that extends the concept of horse whispering, dog whispering, and pizza whispering, and the always popular money whispering. A "ring whisperer" version of this can be observed as a major character trait of Golum, the character in the Hobbit. This can be used continuously through the match or applied only during tense and difficult playing situations.

In this exploitation of your gullibility, the pool hustler addresses his cue stick as if it was an actual, real life, thinking, and conversing entity. The stick has a name (let's use "Jack" as an example). He talks to Jack, carries on conversations, makes and listens to comments, and asks and answers questions. And, just as if Jack was a real person, does all this right in front of you.

The effectiveness of this ploy depends on twinging your curiosity enough to make his actions interesting. He needs to put on enough of a theatrical presentation that you are almost forced to pay attention.

It doesn't really matter whether you believe he has escaped the care of a mind doctor or if someone accidently left his door unlocked. His well-crafted presentation and apparent reality can still drag you into his world.

His side of the verbal communications will be spoken in a normal tone of voice. The other side of the conversations (from Jack) is always covered up with an appropriate length of silence. Only our whisperer has the keen ear and mental wavelength to pick up Jack's responses.

An amateur could not pull this off with any degree of believability. This shark requires a total mental and personal commitment. There are several techniques to accomplish this and to make the effort more believable.

One technique extends the (for some) morning "talking to your face in the mirror". Another easy process is the "imaginary friend" mindset. If he breaks cover even for a sentence, the entire effort is wasted and he is in danger of being laughed out of the pool hall.

During the match, Jack is treated as a coach and advisor. Shot choices and options are discussed, and advice offered. On misses and mistakes, the conversations revolve around solutions to fix the problem, apply different tactics, and on and on.

He can even use this hustle to apply other sharks. For example, he can make comments and jokes to Jack about your clothes, shot choices, shooting results. He can find Jack's "statements" to be hilariously funny – loudly responding.

His normal competition conversations to you are something like, "Jack wants to know if we are solids or strips." "Jack says that's a foul." "Jack thinks you could have made a better shot choice." etc.

If you talk to him directly, he responds normally, although he can sometimes say, "Jack's opinion is ..." He responds for himself and as Jack's interpreter. And when the match is over and the stick put away in its case, Jack is no longer part of the conversation and the hustler appears to be a normal personality.

Response

You would think that if you ignored his antics that the pool hustler would soon get tired of his performance and allow the effort to disappear. An inexperienced amateur trickster would probably wind down the attempt since you aren't paying attention. But an expert gamesman carries on. Its wide flexibility makes it very useful.

A passive response can be applied – but that gives him tacit permission to push the boundaries of table courtesy. This is fine as long as he doesn't converse over your playing time.

You can be proactive. One tactical response would be to interrupt the conversations. Here are some examples:

- "How did you hook up with such a loser?"

- "Doesn't it bother you when he doesn't use you right? "

- "Does it hurt when he puts you together?"

Use your imagination.

Storyteller

Many people enjoy telling stories about their experiences (real and imagined) to any interested audience. Good storytellers are always entertaining and fun to listen. A well-crafted and presented tale is almost always welcome. Narratives can range from short, quick and humorous anecdotes through to the longer tall stories with mini-adventures that build to an interesting conclusion.

A pool hustler who has a talent for storytelling can use this very creatively during a competitive match. He probably has a personality that can't stop performing. A pool match is an excellent opportunity since you are a captive audience of one. There may also be railbirds who can selectively become an audience. Stopping him probably requires rope, a gag, and a couple of assistants.

An amateur hustler doesn't understand the necessity of good presentation and timing. If he's really bad, all he accomplishes is a reputation for rambling nonsense.

An experienced gamesman applies his storytelling skills at two levels. The first level is to be a continuous distraction. If he can reduce your focus enough to miss a few shots during a match, which can be all he wants to do. The second level is the timing of his best stories or jokes – usually when you most desperately need to buckle down and apply all of your concentration on winning.

He might make minor concessions to normal table courtesies – i.e., not talking when you shoot, etc. He might advance a story between your shots. But he also is talking while he shooting. Beginning from the moment he takes over the table, his mouth continues talking – pretty much on automatic. He knows his stories so well, that it doesn't affect his abilities to analyze table layouts and make good shot choices. He might, momentarily, stop talking while he aims and strokes the shot.

The hustler, as an expert storyteller, uses this shark very purposely. He is fully aware that when you are paying attention to his stories, you are also distracted from playing your best game. He can, when you have to make the right shot choice, ensure that part of his storytelling occurs just when you come to the table. The effort to move your attention from his story into the mindset to do a proper table analysis takes time also burns up some of your brain energy. This means you lose valuable thinking time needed to consider multiple options.

If he does an effective job of modifying your will to win, the level of importance originally intended for the match is reduced. The game becomes more of a casual, pass-the-time-of-day effort instead of the deadly serious duel to the death attitude needed to win. As long as he can keep you from thinking carefully, that is all the edge he needs.

Response

It's always enjoyable to listen to a good story. But in a match, you must devote the whole of your thinking to the game. Only this level of focus ensures that good and proper decisions can result in your best chances to win.

You can use the moderately active response of using the hand up, palm out, traditional "stop" signal when you are shooting. When used, hold that pose until he stops talking. Then restart your game. Repeat as needed. Unfortunately, this requires continuous attention to every time he starts talking.

There is a high-road approach that might help stop this shark. Begin with a courteous and firm request that he not talk while you are shooting. If he is unintentional on affecting your game, simply telling stories as a matter of personality, this would work. If he is an evil-doing mind-bender, any agreements are void 15 minutes later.

The low-road approach is more effective. If he is a storytelling addict, you can trick him into losing. Whenever he starts a story, be very encouraging and appreciation. The effect of having an interested listener encourages him to put more passion into his delivery. This gets him to self-shark (always a nice turnaround).

Another tactic is to ask questions about the storyline. For example, "And then what?" "What does <character> do next?" "Are you sure that is what happened?" Continuous interruptions cause confusion and handicap his efforts, with little effect on you.

Sympathy

This is a very common shark. In fact, many players don't consider this to be a shark – just part of the normal competition environment. It is used so often, that this tactic seems to be embedded into normal pool playing culture in barrooms and pool halls across the world. Most players use this routinely. When informed that it is a sharking trick, they would deny this vehemently. You might even be asked if you aren't defining sportsmanship too narrowly.

Here is how the pool hustler applies this shark in competition. Early in the match, he sets the condition of his talking during your turn with compliments on successful efforts. No compliment is too minor. He must first establish his "right" to speak after you make a shot. Once his verbosity is considered acceptable, he can implement this shark.

Very quickly, usually around the second or third game of a match, he does not limit himself to the simple "good shot" statement. He is a bit wordier, adding on an additional qualifying sentence. This starts as a dual compliment - for example, "Good shot. You are on target today." or "Pretty good. You are going to make it tough for me to keep up."

At the mid-game point of the match is when he can begin modifying his comments, and including statements about a few unsuccessful efforts. He assumes the normal sober sorrow and apologetic demeanor that a supporter or an ally would have upon identifying a failure to perform. His considerate words are offered like this:

- *First,* "That was a good try." *Sympathetic put-down,* "Maybe if you used a couple more practice strokes."

- *First,* "You almost made that work." *Sympathetic put-down,* "Don't hurry the shot and take your time."

- *First,* "Aw, man. You were robbed." *Sympathetic put-down,* "That should have been yours."

- *First,* "I wish I could give you a do-over." *Sympathetic put-down,* "You don't deserve to lose from such a small error."

- *First,* "You almost had that." *Sympathetic put-down,* "I think you didn't follow through properly."

- *First,* the Maxwell Smart trademark line "Missed it by that much." *Sympathetic put-down,* "Maybe if you adjusted your stance."

Players on the receiving end of this shark are usually too deeply mired in disappointment. They don't recognize the two-edge, two-faced sympathetic responses to shooting failures.

You missed a shot and now he's at the table - AND, he is sympathetic to the miss - AND mashes your face into your lack of success. You suffer personal disappointment, and have to hear his sympathetic remarks. After a half dozen times or so, you might start considering suicide – and he walks away with the match.

Response

Key to handling this shark is to quickly recognize it. One proactive approach is to put excessive effort in thanking him ever so much for caring about you. Be over-enthusiastic and more than a little sarcastic. An experienced hustler spots when this trick isn't working and stops it (and begins another tactic). An amateur wannabe takes a while to get the message. Make a big deal about it, so that his failure distracts his game.

One of the nice things about attempts of sharking is that you have just received his tacit approval to use sharks during the match. You can push the same trick back at him, with more applied enthusiasm and more details sympathetic statements. This is not going to directly help your game. If successful, he is the one whose game disintegrates.

For example, here is a standard proactive response, "So close, yet so far. You really could use some practice on that shot. I know this instructor who can help you with that problem."

When he starts sending glares of irritation or starts hitting the balls harder than usual, you are succeeding. If possible, make additional sympathetic statements with a bright and cheerful smile. The occasional, "thank you for helping me" also helps.

Table Critic Advisor

This is another hustling trick that is common in most pool playing environments where the pool tables are not in excellent condition. It is commonly used against a player who is playing on the tables for the first time. The shooter might be a regular at another place but is checking out new places and players. Or he could be traveling and just happened to find this place. Of course, this does make you a new "victim" for the resident pool hustler.

This example describes how you could be sharked on an unfamiliar pool table. All tables have some condition problems – even the very best tables. And, face it, there are way too many pool tables that are in mediocre or even pool condition. The table conditions are unknown to you – and known to your pool hustling opponent. Regardless, it's the match table of the moment.

If you are an experienced player who has played on many different tables, you know there are some table conditions to be discovered. You might even have a few ball rolling routines to identify table problems. Nonetheless, your opponent is the home player and familiar with the place.

The hustler starts this shark by being the perfect helpful sportsman - sharing with you details on the table's problems. He opens with, "There's a few things about this table you should know about." He points out that on a slow roll, there are several areas on the table where the ball goes off line. He can point out a couple bad rail areas. He also gives you the secrets of the local workarounds.

Of course, he holds back on a couple table faults. When you discover them (which of course, helps you miss the shot), he apologizes and says something like, "Oh, yeah. I forgot about that."

The purpose of this shark is to fill your head with all of the possible table problems and conditions. This is to direct your attention and focus away from strategies and tactical options.

After a game or two, while you are absorbing this information and making adjustments to your shooting options, he "helpfully" piles on more information. Some examples are:

- "The 1 ball has a chip, and the 4 ball has several nicks."

- "The cue ball sometimes rolls lop-sided." (This can actually be a lie – but anything that forces you to shoot differently is good for him.)

- "The rack makes it impossible to get a tight grouping of balls. Make sure you use this corner for the head ball. It's marked with a piece of tape."

- "There is a dead cushion right there that makes banks impossible, no matter how hard you hit the object ball."

- "Be careful with the mechanical bridge. It has a sharp edge on one of the grooves that can damage your stick."

By mid-match, you are tracking about 20 different table defects. With his helpful input, you are considering every possible problem (roll off, slow cloth, object ball throw, etc.). All of this mental work is on top the usual problems of picking speed, spin, and aim.

These additional concerns to be factored into each shot can make the effort extremely complicated. This is the state of mind the hustler wants you to experience.

Response

Always be suspicious of anyone volunteering information. As a general rule in any pool game, volunteered information should always be suspect. Whatever is offered, be courteous and thank him for his contribution to your knowledge.

Regardless of any input, depend only on your own tests and examinations. Instead, concentrate on how he plays. Those observations tell the truth. Make shooting adjustments based on these discoveries.

Even if some initial information is verified as good, you can't trust him not to insert a false tidbit at a later time. Proceed at your own best speed without dependence on your opponent.

Team Tricks

Just about every pool hall participates in some sort of amateur league teams program that plays several nights a week. The group might be a local pool hall league, or a part of a national league setup (APA, BCA, ACS, etc.) The rules generally support good sportsmanship, but there is a lot of room for sharks to sneak in beneath the radar.

In addition to the many individual sharks which are basically one-on-one efforts, some teams develop their own sharks based on available talents. Two of the most common of these are listed here with the appropriate responses.

In any league, there are always a few captains who intentionally put a great amount of effort in establishing a group of team sharks. They even go so far as holding training sessions to teach members how and when to act. These captains also coach individual players on effective sharking tricks to use against opponents, including what tricks work best against which opponents.

Most captains prefer to maintain (and enforce) good sportsmanship. It's simply a better moral position to maintain. If one of their members attempts to use sharking tricks, the captain comes down immediately (and hard) on the offender. When sportsmanship is discussed among team captains, these are the shining examples on how to properly compete.

The following two examples (with responses) are most commonly observed among league teams. When encouraged by a team captain, these can be quite effective in improving team scores – and can make the difference between a season win (or loss).

Cheerleader

This is the member with the greatest amount of "team spirit". He sits there, watching every shot of every game and is the single most vocal and active supporter of the team. Successful shots by his teammate are followed by loud exclamations of joy and support. Unsuccessful shots evoke exhortations to do better on the next inning.

On a miss by the opposing player, he whoops it up and challenges his team mate to do his best on his new turn at the table. On a game win, there seems to be no limit of his exuberance. He does not directly boo or hiss the opposing player, but he visually enjoys the opportunity to support his team mate. Occasionally, the team captain provides low-voiced suggestions on timing and enthusiasm levels. This may result in toning down his team member support and increasing joyfulness over opposing team player misses and mistakes.

Response

Pay very close attention to the timing of the verbal support. On any situation where the cheerleader looks like he is pushing the edges of intruding on your teammate's turn at the table, immediately jump in and get the opposing team captain to put a lid on his guy.

Annoying Voice

This is a team member with an irritating, loud, intruding, Jerry Lewis-like voice. It penetrates any jukebox music. It slices through conversations within 25 feet. It is unavoidable and a constant factor the whole night long. Added to that, the owner is outgoing, striking up conversations with everyone that comes near. Just being near the match table affects anyone not used to hearing such unpleasant audio vibrations.

His team buddies tune him out easily while playing a match. To your team, who are not acclimated to such a voice, it intrudes across every moment he is speaking. He doesn't even have to be close by your match table. Any conversation within hearing distance disturbs your teammate's analysis and shooting routine. Like the Cheerleader, the team captain is close by to provide timing guidance.

Cheerleader Response

There is not much you can do until this person somehow steps over the boundaries of pool hall behavior. For example, get too loud, or say something wile your teammate is shooting – that is enough to claim foul to the opposing captain. If you need to ask twice, be very vehement. That should keep him under control.

Temper Tantrum

Generally, the "volume" of verbosity and threat-level used by a person implementing this method is pretty much social class-dependent. For example, members of the upper class maintain more control over their temper in social situations, but can still manage a glowering intensity.

Participants in the middle-class are much more verbal. (Witness the parents of players at school sporting events.) The extreme-threat type is more often found frequenting business locations with copious alcohol and low-quality furniture and tables that need major make-overs.

The hustler who uses this tactic must be a consummate actor, able to display emotions in full Technicolor. The entire trick is implemented with cold-hearted calculation.

This trick emulates the behavior and actions of people who are easily irritated and frustrated by anything that complicates their goals and intentions. This includes emotional responses to game losses, even missed shots.

The purpose of this trick is to take your attention and focus off of the pool game and add additional worries about the responses and reactions of your opponent. It also adds a certain amount of wariness about your opponent. All of this affects your playing attitude and rhythm.

The justification for displaying a temper is not the personal fault of the shooter. It is always someone or something else. This makes the shark usable for many occasions. He can use the table, balls, mechanical bridge, even his cue as the reason for a failed shot.

This is a cumulative effort, getting stronger and more noticeable with each occurrence. The first target of the blame game is the equipment. Depending on how this affects your game, he can stay with this level for some time.

When the effect wears off and you start getting control of your game, he expands the targets of his frustration. Depending on the necessary shock required, he can adjust the volume of his tantrum. All of this is carefully calculated based on your reactions. If you are a nervous type, he doesn't need much volume.

When the game reaches the critical point – a key middle-game in the match, or during the end-games, he adjusts his temper tantrum volume to destabilize your concentration.

He could even max out with actual (or strongly implied) threats of physical intervention. Even if you think he might be bluffing, you can't be sure. Any player seemingly in the throes of this kind of emotional upset is unpredictable.

Response

Unfortunately, there are some players who actually descend into insanity during even the most minor of problems. A missed shot, lost game, lost bet – anything could trigger bad behavior.

If real-world, when things start getting intense, you need to consider his capability to invade your personal comfort zone. A lot depends on how much he shreds his self-control.

The first order of business in a situation like this is to evaluate the threat to your well-being. On sober reflection, make a decision as to your next action based on the potential consequences. Depending on his aggressiveness (and how many friends he has in the vicinity), you can:

- Escalate the situation into a knock-down, drag-out fight.

- Quit, gather your stuff and walk away.

- Win the match and expect/hope to leave the premises intact.

- Wimp down and let him win.

If you think this might be a pool hustler's trick to win some easy money, feel free to assume any emotional demonstrations are bluffs and have some fun seeing just how extensive his acting abilities truly are.

But if this was a brush with fate, think over the circumstances that lead to you being in the presence of an unpleasant adversary. It might make good sense to develop some personal rules to prevent future repetitions. And, maybe design a few options to gracefully extract yourself.

Thinker

All pool hustlers have a library of sharks based on different tactics. Many sharks can be categorized. There are a large group of conversation-based sharks and another group based on delaying tricks. The "Thinker" shark is one of those delaying sharking tactics.

It is especially useful in competition environments that restrict direct communications between the players. The most common of these are formal tournaments. Players have designated seats to wait their turns. This is also common in some private pool rooms designed to discourage inter-player communications.

Potential targets for the "Thinker" shark are methodical players. These are shooters who enjoy the Green Game because of the in-turn playing routines, combined with the consistent shooting rhythms (table analysis, shot selection, set up, execution, and maybe a bit of post-shot consideration of the consequences). Methodical players are very sensitive to interruptions in their routines. The pool hustler only needs to modify his victim's timing and playing rhythm to reduce that player's focus and concentration.

This shark takes the table analysis segment of every shooting routine and uses it to affect your thinking. If you are one of these methodical players, this trick interferes with your normal expectations of the game flow. Doing this a few times doesn't have much of an effect on your game. But, over the length of a match, there is a cumulative effect. By the time the match enters the end-games, every time the hustler shoots, the delay has become just a bit more irritating. This affects your state of mind, which, of course, helps the hustler win.

Here is how this is used in a competition. Your opponent's turn comes up. He walks over to the pool table and stops stock still in a statue-like position for a lengthy amount of time. The position can be in a variety of poses. It might be a dignified "English gentleman" – one hand on chin. He might use the "spread-eagle" pose – feet apart, leaning onto the short rail with both hands. He might even use the "edge of the table, half-butt".

He holds this position for a long time. With no formal time per shot, this can extend out beyond 60 seconds and longer. This pose is held until you actually say something. Upon which moment you have just told him the limits of your patience.

From that point onwards, this is his benchmark. He knows that, as the match proceeds, your cumulative frustration increases.

During a long match, he has some options. For example, he might temporarily stop this shark to determine your focus recovery time. He can use it two or three times in a row – or every other shot. With this information, he can control the level of your competitiveness.

He isn't wasting time while in his pose. If you look closely, you can see his eyes darting all over the table area as different ideas are considered and discarded. This shark also gives him the time to evaluate dozens of ideas, concepts, options, and considerations. Even if he makes a shot decision in the first few seconds of his Thinker pose, he can still continue evaluations of options.

When he finally moves past the pose, the actual setup, execution and post-shot analysis doesn't take much time – less than 10 seconds. Then the whole process starts over again. Even if he is strongly pressured and cuts the time in half, you are still waiting longer than you consider practical – and are already frustrated.

Response

Here is the best solution to handling this shark. Use this trick against the hustler. This is an excellent opportunity to improve your thinking game. While he is doing his table analysis, you can also give serious consideration to a wide variety of "what if" scenarios.

Watch him carefully as he studies the playing situation. See if you can identify his options. Try to predict the final choice, and then compare his plan of attack to what you consider the correct selection. If your choice is incorrect – figure out what he was trying to accomplish. It can be very beneficial to know how he makes shooting choices. At the least, you get an insight into how effective his choices are compared to yours.

Time-outs

If you watch any amount of professional football and basketball, this trick is used very often. One team gets on a roll and just cannot do anything wrong. The other team calls a time out. And, so often (not necessarily always), the scoring momentum dies when play is resumed.

In pool, you have experienced time periods when you were in the "groove", playing in the "zone". You get down on the shot to start your inning and suddenly the table is cleared. You make the break, pocket a ball, and you just go on, sinking balls and getting shape with seemingly no effort. Even when you miss, on coming back to the table, the balls drop like rain.

If your opponent lives his sportsmanship, he silently suffers as you advance steadily towards the match win – even though it is a minor form of torture. High standards of sportsmanship require him to be very complimentary about playing so well.

But when your opponent is a pool hustler, he is not the slightest bit interested in sportsmanship. He seriously wants to win, and so takes immediate steps to short-circuit your "zone" playing. He only needs to nudge, push, or shove you out of that groove to get your game back to "normal".

One of the easiest tricks to use is to make a show out of leaving the playing area. He can do this while you are shooting, or during an inning change.

First, he'll busy himself for a minute making his area neat, and then stand up, stretch, and then walk away. If you are still shooting, he only needs you to notice his departure. If it's his turn (especially when he has not shot), he asks for a break. Here are several rhythm-breaking choices:

- Goes to the bathroom and stays there for at least five to ten minutes.

- Goes to the bar to order a drink and just happens to meet a long-lost buddy on the way back.

- Gets in an animated conversation with someone else, and then asks you to wait a minute while he continues talking.

- Goes over to another pool table to watch someone else shoot.

Of course, game play must pause to await his re-appearance. If you are a kindly pool player, you nod acceptance to his request to depart, and wait for his return. If you are shooting, his urgent need to a bathroom break is "reasonable", and out of courtesy, you stop shooting. You settle down for what should be a short wait.

What he has done is put you in a holding pattern. If you can restart shooting within a couple minutes, you can probably continue going well – but he won't allow that. That's why he extends the normal time to several minutes. He needs you to get slightly irritated over the match delay. And that is when your groove flattens out to "normal" playing.

Response

Unless there is a specified limit in the competition rules, there isn't much you can do to stop him. However, there is a passive way and an active response you can take.

The passive approach allows him to proceed with this trick. First of all, do NOT settle down in your chair and attempt to patiently await his return. With your stick in hand, return to the table. Mentally pick up the game and starting playing the table with your imagination.

Where the cue ball would stop, you go over play from there. Get down on the shot and take practice strokes for each cue ball position. Mentally play the game through to the win. This keeps your head focused on playing. When he finally return, it is very easy to pick up your zone and continue winning.

The active approach is very useful when you have a two or three game lead. As he leaves the playing area, walk with him. If he goes to the restroom, you are conversing with him as he attempts to take a leak. If he goes to the bar, you order a soda or water. Stick close. If he talks with someone, you are there, hanging on his shoulder, being the considerate listener.

Waiting to play

These are a number of smaller tricks that a pool hustler can use against you, even while you are at the table and he is waiting to play. All he needs to do is set up a waiting area (usually down table) and perform little activities, seemingly unrelated to you. These little distractive activities are very common among amateur hustlers.

An experienced gamesman usually uses other tools. However, if he notices that you are hyper-aware, this are very easy to apply – and coming from a good player can even be done while seemingly unintentional.

These tricks are designed to provide background "noise" to your concentration on the game's strategies and tactics. Even the occasional recognition that he is doing some kind of movement interferes with your game thinking.

Here is how the hustle works. First, he stakes out his personal waiting location near the foot of the table. This means that during half of your shots, he is visible to your eyeballs, either directly in your line of sight, or well within your peripheral vision.

You can't really say he is directly sharking you, since he is performing these little gimmicks whether you are facing him or not. A person who is unfamiliar with how gamesmanship affects focus and intention would pass off these actions as simple personal habits.

Here are some examples.

- Flipping any small object from hand to hand.
- Squirming in place.
- Leaning slowly over to one side.
- Apparently dozing off, and then jerking upright.
- Leaning the cue stick slowly over to one side.
- Scratching (everywhere from crotch to back).
- In-place jerky movements (if music is playing).

- Motions of encouragement - thumbs up, double-thumbs up, nods, and smiles, with the occasional "Whoo, whoo." thrown in.

- Cue maintenance activities with various tools.

- Using the cell phone, quietly of course, but with animation.

Response

For the more obvious distractive movements, at a tournament you can inform the tournament director who can issue a warning. In a league match, discuss the problem with your captain and ask that he talk to the opposing team captain.

For the more subtle movements, the passive approach would be to live with the situation. To do this, place all of your attention only within the boundaries of the pool table. Anything outside this rectangle simply doesn't exist. You could actively ask him to refrain, but that would not be a long-term solution. A hustler would simply stop for several innings, and then start with subtle actions.

In a casual match, the simplest way to stop him from using this shark would be to threaten to stop playing. An experienced hustler recognizes that this trick is not working. He simply switches over to another shark, so make sure to keep your guard up.

In a bar situation, use the two-step approach. First, loudly enough to be heard by the railbirds, request that he stop his actions. Then, identify one or two of the more drunk onlookers and ask them to watch him closely.

At the very least, this intimidates the amateur wannabe. Such public exposure easily embarrasses him into stopping. (And sometimes the unexpected notoriety distracts him enough to give you an easy win.)

If nothing else works, the absolute last resort is to simply pack up your stick and walk away. Ignore any current bets. There are lots of other places to play that don't include majorly stupid players. You don't need the aggravation.

Waive the Penalty

It's hard to believe that this pool shark actually works so effectively. The trick is simple and straight-forward. The pool hustler apparently decides to give you an unexpected gift. It starts when you have committed some kind of foul. It might be an accidental touch or movement of an object ball, or a similar accidental tip to ball touch or hand/clothing touch to the cue ball. The foul must occur during the shot setup and before a complete stroke is made.

When most fouls are committed, the usual penalty is loss of turn and cue ball in hand for the incoming shooter. For most players, the moment that a foul is committed, it is self-recognized.

You, as the offending player, usually have an immediate moment of realization. A stupid, silly, and dumb, dumb, dumb error was made – by you. This is quickly followed by the dead certainty that your idiotic mistake has just handed the game to your opponent.

Cue ball foul –Whether you or your opponent declares the foul is immaterial. When you know you did it, you know it. This trick works even if the foul has to be pointed out to you.

Most opponents gleefully take over the cue ball and table regardless of the layout, no questions or thinking required. But the pool hustler makes an intermediate analysis based on the table layout. If the ball positions favor him with an easy runout, he simply takes the ball in hand and proceeds to run out the table.

However, if the table layout provides limited opportunities for an immediate win – or if it is still in the early-game, he can "afford" to be generous. Instead of taking up the cue ball, he says (in a kindly tone of voice), "Don't' worry about it. Go ahead, shoot." If questioned why, he waves off any need for an answer and tells you to get on with the shot. Even if queried about the legality of giving up the forfeiture, he says something similar to, "There is no rule that says I have to accept it."

When you realize that you've been granted a momentary exemption, your first reaction is an immediate sense of relief. The billiard gods, through the agency of your opponent has just given you billiards forgiveness. Between the realization of committing a foul and then the sudden charity from your opponent, your concentration is going to be frazzled. For a short period of time, that disorientation about the rules of the universe affects your thinking and shooting abilities.

If you committed the foul and picked up the cue ball to offer it, the pool hustler still has to validate the correct decision – take it or not. If he does accept the cue ball and runs out to the win, he is very apologetic that he had to do that to you. But if he decides it in his best interest to appear kind and forgiving, he just says to place it where you think is right – and get on with the game.

Object ball touched - If this is not a penalty like the cue ball foul, you only need to shift the balls back into place and get his verbal approval. At the very least, this act of carelessness is a bit embarrassing (and distracting to your concentration). To further frazzle your already confused mindset, he can make it worse by making a generous allowance – even to the point of allowing the balls to lay as they are with no adjustment.

Response

There is no advantage for you to accept any seemingly generous waiver of the rules, whether you think you gain an advantage or not. The affect it has on your game focus and concentration is simply not worth accepting such seemingly kind offers of forgiveness. Accepting the first time can lead to mental complacency. If you were given a gift once, then on a future foul you are semi-expecting the same generosity. If not forgiven, you suffer a certain amount of irritated frustration – which benefits him. It is not worth any temporary gain you get.

If you refuse the offer the first time, there is one additional possible distraction he can get from this trick. He can continue to offer it, up to the point where you get pissed off. He then gracefully withdraws from the effort – with the knowledge that you are now playing with an irritation. This is a very good way to force you to play badly. If this case, from your chair with a smile on your face, thank him and ignore his requests. This can actually frustrate him – which benefits you.

Minor Sharks

Experienced pool hustlers use a lot of tricks. Many of them have been honed over years of practice and stored away into a personal library of gamesmanship. Their efforts are intended to subtract as many percentage points off of your normal shooting skills as possible. The "lessening" of your table abilities is all that is needed to win.

Wannabe hustlers are much easier to spot. Any railbird with knowledge of pool strategies and tactics and with a minimal recognition of sharking tricks can easily spot their efforts. Whether railbirds want to inform the "victim" is debatable.

Just an FYI (for your information) – most railbirds do not want to get involved in helping one player over another – even when such mental tactics are recognized. A lot of these dedicated observers of the game also believe that the inclusion of gamesmanship in table billiards is a necessary element of competition. If they like placing side bets with others, they simply adjust the odds to suit themselves. Never underestimate the observation skills of railbirds.

Many of these minor sharks are often seen among lesser skilled players (bar-bangers) in bars. They are usually done, not as intentional distractions, but simply their understanding of their local pool "culture". These are often just unconscious behavior, picked up by watching other players and adopted as part of the way the game is played.

Advance Notice

This shark is very popular among amateur golfers. It has migrated into the pool room because it has been so effective in making shooters less able to concentrate on winning.

It begins during the introductions at the beginning of a competition. The hustler informs you that he is going to shark you during the match. This actually is very effective if you've had a couple of beers when your thinking isn't too sharp.

He will, in an apologetic tone, inform you that he is occasionally accidently or absent-mindedly discourteous - and by the way would you please forgive him in advance. Here are several requests that he could be asking for your advanced forgiveness:

- "Sometimes I get so wrapped up in the game that I forget myself. I might absentmindedly walk in front of you while you are shooting."

- "Sometimes I forget whose turn it is. Let me know when I do that and I will back off."

- "I have a cough tonight. I will do my best to suppress it and not interrupt your game."

- "I am expecting an important phone call. I hope that it doesn't distract you."

As a result, you enter the competition knowing that you are going to be sharked. This creates the expectation that it happens, plus you are wondering when it will be repeated. He doesn't even have to do any of these. With the anticipation alone he has thrown you off your game.

Response

You have to realize immediately that this is a trick. To handle it, first thank him for the pre-notification. You can respond in two ways: Say that you too have this problem and often come to stand close to the table, directly in front of him during his turn. Use a bright smile. The second possible response is: "Sorry about that. I too have a problem. A couple months ago, I lost your temper and physically injured someone who intentionally sharked me. I hope you don't mind."

Am I in your way?

In many pool halls, the tables are spaced away from the wall so there is just enough distance for a person to shoot normal shots. But often times, chairs and stools are aligned along the wall for railbirds and players to sit in. When a shooter plays from that side of the table, courtesy usually requires the seated person to move without being asked.

This situation offers an easy shark opportunity by the seated person. If he is a team member or a supporter, he can intentionally affect your concentration for the upcoming shot. He simply needs to stay in his chair when you come around table and get into position for the shot. As soon as you recognize that he is blocking or restricting your shot, you are forced to stop the setup, turn around, and say something. This alone is usually sufficient to distract.

Sometimes, he gets the jump on you just as you turn. With an innocent tone of voice, he asks, "Am I in your way?" When you agree, he slowly removes himself from the area. Or, just as you turn, without the conversation, he makes a big production out of moving himself aside.

Either way, he has forced your attention off the table, destroyed any tactical plans you were considering, and modified your game rhythm. With the shooting limitation seemingly resolved, you now have re-gather your focus and attention and get back into the game.

Response

As you approach the place where you need to set up, and notice that someone is not being courteous, you can get good results by first stepping on a foot. Apologize profusely. Then, to add insult to injury, get down on the shot (before he can move) and jam your butt right into his face. If he doesn't desperately scramble away to escape confronting your backside, he certainly does so in the future if it even looks like you might consider shooting from that side of the table. The one example should be enough of a lesson to any others who might consider this trick.

Annoyances

Many people have habits or personal traits that are annoying. The degree of irritation suffered is dependent on the observer. Such irritants are frustrating enough in the normal world of work and family. But in the pool hall, their effective is enhanced by the environment. Nonetheless, these all affect how well you can concentrate on winning.

An experienced hustler, using this tactic has to quickly identify the most effective annoyances. As each "social grace" is presented, your reaction is closely monitored. Sometimes he gets lucky and finds two or even three annoyances that bother you. Once discovered, he utilizes them at important or critical situations when their performance causes the greatest impact on your state of mind.

Any of these tactics, when use by an amateur, are simply bad habits. Here is a short list that has been observed in pool halls:

- Talks on a cell phone - loudly and with great enthusiasm.
- Shares everything about his personal life.
- Greets or waves at everyone that comes close to him.
- Slurps on the straw of an empty cup of soda - multiple times.
- Doesn't cover mouth when coughing.
- Flips coins while waiting for you to finish your turn.
- Wears too much cologne or perfume.
- Throws trash on the floor, then uses his foot to push under a chair.
- Eats sunflower seeds and tries to throw the shells in a trash container six feet away.
- Chews food with mouth open, occasionally letting some fall out.
- Clips and cleans fingernails with meticulous attention.
- Always starts sentences with "You know." and "What?"
- Blows nose with noisy intent.

- Doesn't use deodorant, but performs the "wave" at every success.
- Forgets your name - and hems and haws as he then remembers the wrong name.

- Stares at you fixedly, never taking his eyes off of you (or some body part).
- Farts loudly, and pretends it was someone else.
- Picks nose and inspects the captured contents.
- Sniffles his way through a cold.
- Harrumphs with intent, and then spits on the floor.
- Clicks a retractable pen, in a race to see how many he can click in one minute.
- Wears sunglasses and a backwards baseball cap.
- Picks his teeth and checks to see if a tidbit came out to become a snack.
- Never makes eye contact.
- Chews on a pencil or pen, sideways.
- Shakes hands with a limp wrist and while leaning slightly away.
- Shakes with his left hand, saying his right was touched by an angel.
- Speaks in a terrible accent, that changes minute to minute.
- Acts like he is drunk - but only orders sodas.
- Pretends to be slightly deaf, and speaks too loud too.
- Cracks his knuckles in time to music.
- Speaks so quietly you have to ask for a repeat.
- Calls you "Kid" or "Son" if you are younger.
- Calls you "Old Man" if you are older.
- Calls you "chief" or "buddy" or something other than your name.

Responses

An amateur with any of these bad habits cannot easily be stopped. It's not as if you could simply walk up to him and slap him silly. Loudly complaining that he is using such and such a shark to distract you gets some attention - usually strange looks and inquiries about your mental health.

However, you can tease him about any of his displays. Here are a few possible responses:

- Knuckle cracker - "Can you do that to send messages in Morse code?"

- Limp handshake - "A little gay today?"

- Chews on pen/pencil - "Does that come in other flavors?"

- Slightly deaf - walk up closely and speak very loudly and slowly into their ear. "Hooowwww arrrrre yyyoooouuu?"

- Sunglass wearing – "Lights are too bright for you?"

If it irritates you, you need to be pro-active. Teasing and "friendly" insults can help you overcome your frustrations. Applying a moderate sense of humor makes your mind less affected.

Do keep in mind - such responses that you use are for entertainment only. You don't need to add to your list of deadly enemies. There are many idiots out there, some of whom have infiltrated the pool room. You need a minimum level of tolerance, just to ensure that you are not driven crazy.

Concession

A concession is when one player concedes the current pool game to the other player. This, believe it or not, can be used as a shark. Normally, when one player has a simple shot on the money ball, the game can be conceded. This allows the game win to be acknowledged as well as saving time by getting next game started.

Under normal circumstances, this wouldn't be a shark. Here is how it can affect your game. Certain conditions have to be met. First of all, there must be two or three balls left on the table. At least two of them should be fairly easy to make. You know you can run out, but it might be a little tricky. Suddenly, your opponent comes up to the table and states, "That's good for you." He starts racking the balls for the next game.

This immediately affects y our emotions. Not having to shoot to the win is a great relief. It also sets up anticipation that you receive similar concessions in future games.

He has made you mentally prepared to expect generosity – not a good idea about any opponent. On the next game, he simply has to refuse to give the concession and your attitude is affected by this seeming betrayal.

Anything that affects your state of mind (happy or angry) affects your concentration on the next game. And don't forget the distraction caused by the offer. Plus, there is an implication that he expects you to do you a return favor.

Response

Never take gifts from opponents. Get your mind into the game and keep it there. Whether he tries to give you the game win or asks if he has to shoot the last shot – play every game out to the bitter end.

146

Fake 8 Ball Handicap

Here is an 8 Ball sharking trick that is often used on beginning players. It is an easy way for the pool hustler to appear to give a very generous handicap. In reality, he is setting up easy wins.

A fantastic handicap is offered. It begins like this. "I really only play pool for money – but you already know I'm a better shooter than you. How about I give you a handicap?"

The beginner cautiously asks for more information – suspicious of a trick. The hustler continues, "After someone makes their first ball, you can take any three balls off the table. How's that sound?"

And here is where greed overcomes common sense. If still reluctant, the offer goes up to 4 balls off the table. A few "Come on – we're not playing for big bucks – what's to hurt?"

The victim, already dazzled by such a generous handicap, is talked into a few games. Usually, the balls taken off are in clusters or blocked by opponent balls. What he doesn't know is that this actually makes the table very easy to run out.

Carefully managed to allow the occasional win, the pool hustler can spend hours pulling money out of his new cash machine.

Against a pool hustler who is hiding some skills, when the beginner starts showing signs of quitting, the handicap is extended to 5 balls.

Response

If the beginner player is a friend of yours, you could pull him off to the side and warn him of what is happening. If he's a friend, but irritated you recently, you might let him suffer for a few games.

If you're the beginning pool player, select another handicap. For example, making either of your last two balls would win the game.

Another option is payoff differences. If he wins, you pay $1.00. If you win, he pays $5.00. If you get ahead, resist his efforts to change the payoff.

Leading Questions

These are easy sharks for a pool hustler to use against you. These types of questions have the sole purpose of forcing you to stop thinking about the competition and consider an answer to the question. It is used primarily as a distraction when it appears that you have advanced a bit more than your opponent feels comfortable about managing.

Any of these questions inserted into your playing routines create a minor diversion of your attention and focus. Individually they have little impact. A series of these can become more distractive.

- "Have you ever timed your break speed?"
- "Do you focus on the cue ball or the object ball when you shoot?"
- "How slow can you hit the cue ball?"
- "Have you ever played pool on an outdoor table?"
- "How long have you been playing pool?"
- "Is your follow-through always that short?"
- "Where did you buy your cue stick?"
- "Is that a custom or off-the-shelf stick?"
- "What kind of cue tip do you use?"

Response

It would be sensible to politely request that he not speak during your turn. If that doesn't work, use the ignore tactic. Simply treat such questions as simple background noise.

Alternately, turn the questions around back at your opponent. Use ignorance for answer, and then come back with, "What about you?" You can irritate him even more by using follow-up questions. This added tactics further distract him from his game.

My Stick is Better

This is a much more focused effort than the *Equipment* shark. It is designed to compare the quality of your stick against the obviously superior cue stick of your opponent.

At every good shot he makes, he brags up that it is the stick that makes it easy. At every bad shot you do; he blames your stick for causing the problem.

Eventually, these continuous comparisons start putting your attention on your cue stick, rather than on each shot. And, of course, your game starts getting worse. As you shoot worse and worse, you get even more frustrated. Eventually, you no longer have the ability to play effective.

Here are some praises of his equipment:

- "My Bulka is designed to completely eliminate deflection."

- "My cue has a sweet feel when I use low speeds."

- "Did you see the spin on the cue ball? That's the special tip I put on. Cost me $75."

- "Did you see that stop shot? That's the perfect follow through that my stick almost forces me to use."

- "Look at that draw. That's from the perfect curve on my tip."

- "See that break? That's the embedded steel in the cue butt."

He blows off any taunts if he messes up with, "Didn't set up properly," or other similar excuses. But when you miss, he mentions something about sub-standard equipment. When you blow a critical shot, he pounces with comforting words, "You can't help it. It's your stick." Any attempt to defend your equipment only proves that this shark is working.

Response

A reasonably excessive, "Shut up." might work - but, probably not. Instead, politely tell him, "You are just trying to justify throwing away your money." On every bad shot, blame it on his stick. (Extra point if he winces.)

Nagger

Some people, for one reason or another, always want to intrude upon your playing pleasure by offering up little helpful reminders. Some players seem to have a "Mom" complex and love to assume that role – even at the pool table. A number of these are:

- "Don't forget to chalk for every s hot."
- "Stay down on the shot."
- "Always follow through."

The first few times you hear these reminders about good playing and shooting habits won't be too bothersome. But after the first five or six times you are interrupted in your playing rhythm, you start getting irritated. The fifteenth time can generate much more internal anger than the fifth time.

True, some players do this, not with the intent to piss you off, but out of the kindness of their heart. In their mind, they are the Good Samaritan, stumbling upon a poor unfortunate (you) who desperately needs guidance on fundamentals.

They consider themselves helpful and kindly guides. In reality, they are naggers, plain and simple.

Response

In the interests of good sportsmanship, you don't want to fulfill your first impulse to tell this good fellow to simply shut up. The passive response would be to simply accept the recommendations as just another of the many elements of the playing environment. It could be easily ignored, like juke box music.

If you like a more active approach, apply some moderate sarcasm, something like, "Thank you. Without your help I couldn't tie my shoes." A couple of these should indicate that you are not receptive to any kind of suggestions about your game.

Overused Words

Of all the overused words in the world of table billiards, the most common of all is, "Good Shot!" These and other pool phrases have become so common as to have lost all real meaning, from the provider or to the recipient.

Such words can be used as a sharking trick. Here are some examples that, with various emotional efforts can be distractive:

- Good luck.
- It could be worse.
- Better luck next time.
- Be careful.
- Good try.

Besides the varying enthusiasm levels, simply saying these excessively can be irritating – just because you know he is using these sportsmanlike words as a tool to frustrate.

It is the constant repetition that can wear away at your patience like water wears away rocks. A few here or there have little effect, but continuous use eventually cracks your wall of patience.

Response

Recognizing that these words are being used as another distractive tactic makes it easy to discount their value. Simply treating such comments as background noise eliminates their effectiveness.

An active approach would be to return these words back at his shots – but with more enthusiasm. You can even add more words to these to make these "digs" more effective.

Self Talker

Sometimes you get an opponent who does his entire strategic and tactical selections in a conversation with himself. Most people occasionally verbalize their thoughts while making a decision. For example, while driving, they may mutter, "Should I go this way, or that way?" It is a fleeting exposure to their mind set and generally is quickly self-censored.

In this bit of diversion, your opponent begins every turn with a complete situational analysis. Every thought is verbalized for anyone to observe their thinking processes and patterns.

Eventually all gets boiled down to a final argument of "go this way or go that way". Finally, the shot takes place. If successful, the process starts over with all of its attendant delays. If unsuccessful, he returns to the sidelines saying comments similar to, "I should have gone the other way. I'm an idiot.)

This is distractive when you start listening to his words. Normally, it doesn't take much to pull your attention into his analysis – to the detriment of your focus. You should be evaluating the table layout and considering your options, not giving serious consideration to his thinking.

Response

This is almost always an unconscious shark. If so confronted, the denials are vehemently stated. He has probably been doing the same routine for his entire playing career. Even the buddies he plays with are so used to him, his verbal idiosyncrasy is ignored.

His run-on self-conversations can provide an insight into his table analysis. He could provide valuable details about what he considers tough or difficult. He is also describing his entire playing capabilities.

If so inclined, you can have a bit of fun with occasional contributions to his verbal flow.

Start and Stop

If you expect your match to go smoothly through to the completion with a winner (hopefully you) and a loser (hopefully your opponent), this shark can bother you.

On the shot, he sets up and prepares to play a shot, even to the practice strokes. Suddenly, he pauses, seems to think for a moment, and then gets up from the shot and assumes the pose of a statue, staring at the table. After a short period of time, pre-shot routine begins again.

This can think, start, stop process can be used in many ways, including:

- On an occasional shot

- During every shot

- Several times during the same shot.

Response

There's not too much you can do to prevent your opponent from initiating this series of hiccups in the flow of the game.

In a formalized environment – league play, tournaments, etc. – you can invoke the time clock. In an informal environment, requesting that he not delay the game too much might help.

One effective response is to simply walk away from the table. Get a drink, go to the restroom or simply engage someone else in a conversation.

The Gang is All Here

Sometimes you have an opponent who travels as part of a pack, similar to wolves and hyenas. Wherever he goes, they go. They cling together, traveling from place to place. Every locale they enter, they take over and change the atmosphere. With loud and boisterous behavior, they overwhelm any other activities. If the environment was quiet and peaceful, they turn it into a loud, obnoxious party.

When you have to play against someone that belongs to this pack of verbal hooligans, you suddenly discover that you are not playing one person, but the entire group.

When your opponent is playing, everyone shouts and cheers his progress. When you shoot, the mob constantly distracts you. They are particularly insulting when you are trying to shoot. If successful, they shout obscenities and insults.

While gangs like this are generally low class, the lowest level of these groups goes beyond hurling verbal abuse. If you are beating their favorite, your life and limb can be threatened. If there is any amount of money on the game, they perform every type of mental intimidation their little minds can think up.

Response

How you handle a group like this depends on your personality and experience. If you have dealt with such goons before, you can join in on their frivolity, and psych them into getting them to treat you as an equal. If you have a more retiring mindset, you may want to take the first opportunity to escape, with or without your equipment.

Generally, when a gang invades a business establishment, do as much as you can to fade into the background. Turn down invitations to compete by using the "don't know how to play" excuse.

Leave as soon as possible. When you have an opportunity, re-think your reasons for being in such places where a gang or two may use as their hang-out.

Waffler

This is not seen very often, but does show up once in a while. Your opponent goes through the entire pre-shot routine, with practice strokes. Suddenly, he seems to lose confidence in his stroke.

He shifts his bridge hand over to the side and tests the shot with full follow-through. This is repeated several times and the bridge hand is brought back in line with the shot.

A variation of this is to perform the practice strokes, and suddenly stop. He might make a minor adjustment of his bridge hand or the height (follow/draw) of the stoke, and then resume the practice strokes.

Once he gets ready to actually shoot the shot, he seems to be ready to stroke the shot, only to not commit to the stroke. This can be done several times before the shot is actually executed.

If you are closely following his shooting, there is a slight tightening of your muscles as he telegraphs the intent to stroke. When he doesn't do this, there is a small mental reaction.

Doing these several times can exhaust your mental preparedness. These can be unconscious attempts to make sure the stroke is dialed in rightly, and can indicate an obsessive desire to make the shot right.

Response

You might get fooled a few times on this trick. If you allow yourself to pay attention to his shot, you can get distracted.

The easiest way to handle this is by placing your attention elsewhere – even closing your eyes works. Wait for the click of the balls to bring your attention back to the table.

Some Final Words

This book provides tools to prevent the majority of pool hustlers and wannabe hustlers from achieving a shortcut to victory. It is up to you to learn about and become aware of all the various tricks, traps, and sharks that can be used in your sport.

Skill, competence, knowledge, and honed abilities all are necessary for a good competition. But when any player injects various types of psychological trickery into the game, it is important to be able to recognize and stop such attempts.

About Hustlers & Sharking

Money players all use elements of hustling and sharking. From the small change amateur to the big money back-room pool players, they want to win. When money is on the line, these players are focused on winning - period.

Every pool playing gambler has a library of well-practiced skits, presentations, and maneuvers available. They all have a talent for the game, but also know that winners are more often determined by the person with the most skillful use of psychological mind games.

If you do not educate yourself about these activities, you can expect to experience many expensive life lessons. Presented below is a learning technique that provides practical experiences at a relatively low cost.

1. **Find a local money player.** In the local pool hall, hang around enough to be able to recognize the local money players. These are not hustlers in the truest sense of financial disaster, but they all have various strategies designed to "educate" a newbie. Any railbird can point out those who are in at the time.

2. **Dangle the bait.** Appear reluctant to play for anything other than "fun." Negotiate a cheap match (table time, a couple of bucks, a drink, etc.). Play your best, but spend the majority of your attention watching and identifying the style and presentation of the sharks he uses. Even if he's

trying to "hide his speed" while building you up, he unconsciously uses a small variety of sharks. These are the ones he is most familiar with and are as automatic as breathing to him.

3. **Observe the action.** Get in two or three matches until he starts nagging about raising the stakes. By then, he has shown you all of his common mind tricks and a few of his defensive skills too. If possible, play a variety of games (8-ball, 9-ball, one-pocket, etc.) to stretch out the time, and observe his style. When you extract yourself, he should let you go easily, since he knows that you are always around. He expects this to be the first round of (what he hopes) to be a long and profitable relationship.

4. **Repeat with other players.** Use this process at several pool halls. By the time you have played five or six of these players, you have gained a significant amount of information and experience, including identification of the majority of their sharks.

This experiment accomplishes several goals. You are able to:

• Gain experience in money games.

• Realize intelligence can manage greed.

• Use observation to identify useful information.

• Apply psychology as an important part of the game.

• Apply caution in new situations.

• Apply minor sharks of your own.

The whole experiment should take about 3-4 weeks and cost no more than $200. A little bit of pain now to prevent a lot of pain later. These are very cheap lessons indeed. With this experience, you can make smarter choices on the types of competitions you want to get involved with.

How Hustlers Research Victims

Most of those who use gamesmanship tricks and traps (consciously and/or unconsciously) rarely take the time and effort necessary to polish their skills. These amateurs are quite obvious in their efforts.

The expert pool hustler has a library of tested tools. There is a key difference between a dilettante wannabe hustler and an adept gamesman – the necessary research to identify potential adversaries and their abilities. This is done by observing local and regional pool players during practice times and competitions (league matches and tournaments).

Essentially, he creates an internal database of players. First, he has to cull the pool playing population. All the beginners and most intermediates are eliminated from the database. They just won't gamble anything meaningful.

With this reduced population, the ones that like to gamble can be identified. Whatever sorting mechanism the pool hustler uses, here are some of the details that he needs to apply against those players:

- General skill level (e.g., A, B, C or APA 4, 5, 6, 7).

- Background (e.g., years of experience, average weekly playing time).

- Special skills (e.g., banking cross-side or sharp cuts).

- Comfort zones (e.g., up to 30-degree cuts, up to 5 feet distance).

- Chaos zones (e.g., off-the-rail shots, over 6 feet distance shots).

- BPI (e.g., 2, 3, 4 balls per inning average).

- Shooting style (e.g., pre-shot routine, aiming by feel or system).

- Personality (e.g., quick-tempered, patient).

- Strategy/skill levels (e.g., shooting to the opponent, using or even recognizing opponent strategies).

- Tactics/skill levels (e.g., good shot selections/patterns, response to bad layouts).

- Stamina (e.g., can only play effectively about 5-6 games).

Added to this knowledge base, he also identifies each player's favorite sharks and the quality of presentation. He notes the effectiveness against those player's opponents. By knowing what can be expected, counter-sharks can be determined.

Casual conversations with other railbirds provide useful information on local players – especially which ones like to gamble. These individuals will, of course, become his first set of potential targets. Any table time (practicing or pick-up games) do not reveal his true speed.

Most general details can be simply identified from spectator chairs. Whenever practice tables are open, he can watch a player work on specific practice shots. That identifies the shots that are considered problems. This is always good to know information.

On completing his survey, he can then get serious. Depending on his preferences, he can then pick through multiple prospects over a week or so. He can also concentrate on taking down a flush player in a single session.

An experienced gamesman does not over-use his tricks. Because he is only interested in winning the money, sharks are applied when needed.

There are a few hustlers who are not so much interested in hauling in the cash as they are in using their mind games for fun and games. For these players, sharking is more of a hobby.

P.S.

You can expect pool to be enjoyed for your entire lifetime. Knowledge of gamesmanship tactics is very beneficial. It is knowledge of strategies, tailored to the opponent that makes the game more interesting and fun. Good luck and shoot straight.

By the same author ....

These are books written by the author up until the time this book was published. All of these books are available in printed format (online bookstores), PDF (billiardgods.com), Kindle (Amazon), and Nook (B&N).

- Billiards Skills Competition Training Program
- Table Map Library
- Drills & Exercises for Pool & Pocket Billiards*
- Cue Ball Control Cheat Sheets*
- Advanced Cue Ball Control Self-Testing Program*
- Safety Toolbox
- The Art of War versus The Art of Pool
- FAQs of Pool & Pocket Billiards
- The Art of Team Coaching
- The Art of Personal Competition
- The Art of Marketing & Promotion
- The Art of Politics & Campaigning
- Kitchen God's Guide for Single Guys

*translated to other languages

Acknowledgements

A special mention must go to my parents (Edmund & Bernadette Sand) who taught me the value of gamesmanship as a survival tool in the modern-day world.

Other individuals who contributed to the book's contents, in no particular order:

- Matt Sherman
- Bob Jewett
- Eric Harada
- Jerry Hardage
- Mickey Suen
- Ted Mauro
- Carter Adams
- Frank Barnes
- Flo Hendrickson
- Those who tried to shark the author and those who were the author's victims.

WARNING: This book is NOT to be used as an educational instruction book on how to shark other players. Here is why: if you read the book and use some of the tricks in a game, what will happen if the other player (or a friend of the player) recognizes your mind game attempt (and he is either bigger, or has more friends)?

www.ingramcontent.com/pod-product-compliance
Lightning Source LLC
Chambersburg PA
CBHW072013090426

42740CB00011B/2175